Jim G

P9-DZO-311

GEORGE MacDONALD

The Best from All His Works

OTHER AUTHORS IN THE SERIES

Andrew Murray: The Best from All His Works

Charles H. Spurgeon: The Best from All His Works

F. B. Meyer: The Best from All His Works

GEORGE MacDONALD

The Best from All His Works

George MacDonald
Edited by Charles Erlandson

THE
CHRISTIAN
CLASSICS
COLLECTION

THOMAS NELSON PUBLISHERS
Nashville

Copyright © 1988 by Thomas Nelson Publishers

All rights reserved. Written permission must be secured from the publisher
to use or reproduce any part of this book, except for brief quotations in critical reviews or articles.

Published in Nashville, Tennessee, by Thomas Nelson, Inc. and distributed in
Canada by Lawson Falle, Ltd., Cambridge, Ontario.

Printed in the United States of America.

Scripture quotations are from the King James Version of the Bible.

Library of Congress Cataloging-in-Publication Data

MacDonald, George, 1824–1905.
   [Selections. 1988]
   George MacDonald, the best from all his works / edited by Charles
Erlandson.
     p.   cm. — (The Christian classics collection; vol. 1)
   ISBN 0-8407-7438-9
   1. Spiritual life. I. Erlandson, Charles. II. Title.
III. Series.
BV4501.M3382   1988
285.8—dc19   88–22395
                                              CIP

1 2 3 4 5 6 — 92 91 90 89 88

Contents

GEORGE MacDONALD

George MacDonald was born December 10, 1824, at Huntly, Aberdeenshire. He studied at King's College and took his M.A. there in 1845. In 1850 he became a minister in a Congregationalist church in Arundel, but he soon ran into trouble for preaching that unbelievers who died were given a second chance for salvation. MacDonald's congregation reduced his salary, and in 1853 the situation became so intolerable that he resigned from his position.

In the 1850s MacDonald began his career as a writer for which he is most famous. His first success came with an extended dramatic poem, "Within and Without," while he found his true literary genius with the publication of *Phantastes*, an adult fantasy, in 1858. MacDonald devoted the remainder of his life to his literary endeavors, publishing fantasies, fairy tales, poetry, novels, translations, and criticism. MacDonald eschewed external success, and although he found a sizable audience, he was perpetually dependent on benefactors, including Lady Byron, for income until his death on September 18, 1905.

MacDonald's career as a writer led to his acquaintanceships with many prominent authors of his day, including Tennyson, Carlyle, Arnold, Ruskin, and Lewis Carroll, who was close enough to the MacDonald family to be called "Uncle Dodgson" by MacDonald's children. In America MacDonald was acquainted with Whittier, Emerson, and Twain. MacDonald's influence continues to extend into the twentieth century, and he has influenced such prominent twentieth-century authors as G. K. Chesteron, W. H. Auden, Charles Williams, and C. S. Lewis.

Introduction

George MacDonald is known today for his works of fiction. In particular, it is his fantasies and fairy tales that continue to capture the imaginations of his readers. MacDonald turned to novel writing in the 1860s in an effort to support himself by his writing, but his novels are often too ponderous and weighted with preaching. Even C. S. Lewis found that the "texture of his writing as a whole is undistinguished, at times fumbling."

MacDonald's fantasies and fairy tales, however, succeed in awakening a sense of wonder in the reader. In these works MacDonald uses his created worlds to show how reality is full of a meaning and unity that God has given it. As MacDonald himself wrote: "The very outside of a book had a charm to me. It was a kind of sacrament—an outward sign of an inward and spiritual grace; as, indeed, what on God's earth is not?"

Even after MacDonald turned to his literary career he continued to lecture and deliver sermons. Several volumes of his "unspoken sermons" exist, and the themes that are pronounced in his fictional work, for example that God is the source of all life, is echoed in his sermons. One can even find examples of his sermons imbedded in some of his novels.

Rejecting the Calvinism of his parents, MacDonald saw any creedal formulations as too restricting and as ultimately only opinion. As a result MacDonald sometimes presents anamolous interpretations, and occasionally he wanders into heterodoxy, for example regarding the atonement. Nevertheless, MacDonald's sermons often evoke the same sense of wonder in God's creation and its sacramentalism as does his fiction.

"The Light Princess" originally appeared in Mac-Donald's 1864 novel Adela Cathcart. *In this novel a number of symbolic tales are told within the framework of a realistic narrative. In both* Adela Cathcart *and "The Light Princess" MacDonald demonstrates his theory of the healthy effect fairy tales (and all imaginative literature that proceeds from the Christian imagination) have on men.*

Ostensibly "The Light Princess" is the story of a princess whose gravity is taken away from her through the curse of a wicked fairy and the princess's attempts to overcome the effects of this curse. But there is a spiritual meaning here, as in all of MacDonald's fairy tales. In the end, the wicked fairy's curse has a good effect on the princess as she is forced to accept a sacrifice of love. True love, we see, is a giving of one's self, and to live one must die to one's self. Often considered MacDonald's best story, "The Light Princess" was successful from the beginning and has even been made into an animated film.

≈

CHAPTER ONE

The Light Princess

I
What! No Children?

Once upon a time, so long ago that I have quite forgotten the date, there lived a king and queen who had no children.

And the king said to himself, "All the queens of my acquaintance have children, some three, some seven, and some as many as twelve; and my queen has not one. I feel ill-used." So he made up his mind to be cross with his wife about it. But she bore it all like a good patient queen as she was. Then the king grew very cross indeed. But the queen pretended to take it all as a joke, and a very good one too.

"Why don't you have any daughters, at least?" said he. "I don't say *sons;* that might be too much to expect."

"I am sure, dear king, I am very sorry," said the queen.

"So you ought to be," retorted the king; "you are not going to make a virtue of *that,* surely."

But he was not an ill-tempered king, and in any matter of less moment would have let the queen have her own way with all his heart. This, however, was an affair of state.

The queen smiled.

"You must have patience with a lady, you know, dear king," said she.

She was, indeed, a very nice queen, and heartily sorry that she could not oblige the king immediately.

The king tried to have patience, but he succeeded very badly. It was more than he deserved, therefore, when, at last, the queen gave him a daughter—as lovely a little princess as ever cried.

II
Won't I, Just?

The day grew near when the infant must be christened. The king wrote all the invitations with his own hand. Of course somebody was forgotten.

Now it does not generally matter if somebody *is* forgotten, only you must mind who. Unfortunately, the king forgot without intending to forget; and so the chance fell upon the Princess Makemnoit, which was awkward. For the princess was the king's own sister; and he ought not to have forgotten her. But she had made herself so disagreeable to the old king, their father, that he had forgotten her in making his will; and so it was no wonder that her brother forgot her in writing his invitations. But poor relations don't do anything to keep you in mind of them. Why don't they? The king could not see into the garret she lived in, could he?

She was a sour, spiteful creature. The wrinkles of contempt crossed the wrinkles of peevishness, and made her face as full of wrinkles as a pat of butter. If ever a king could be justified in forgetting anybody, this king was justified in forgetting his sister, even at a christening. She looked very odd, too. Her forehead was as large as all the rest of her face, and projected over it like a precipice. When she was angry, her little eyes flashed blue. When she hated anybody, they shone yellow and green. What they looked like when she loved anybody, I do not know; for I never heard of her loving anybody but herself, and I do not think she could have managed that if she had not somehow got used to herself.

But what made it highly imprudent in the king to forget her was—that she was awfully clever. In fact, she was a witch; and when she bewitched anybody, he very soon had enough of it; for she beat all the wicked fairies in wickedness, and all the clever ones in cleverness. She despised all the modes we read of in history, in which offended fairies and witches have taken their revenges; and therefore, after waiting and waiting in vain for an invitation, she made up her mind at last to go without one, and make the whole family miserable, like a princess as she was.

So she put on her best gown, went to the palace, was kindly received by the happy monarch, who forgot that he had forgotten her, and took her place in the procession to the royal chapel. When they were all gathered about the font, she contrived to get next to it, and throw something into the water; after which she maintained a very respectful demeanour till the water was applied to the child's face. But at that moment she turned round in her place three times, and muttered the following words, loud enough for those beside her to hear:—

"Light of spirit, by my charms,
  Light of body, every part,
Never weary human arms—
  Only crush thy parents' heart!"

They all thought she had lost her wits, and was repeating some foolish nursery rhyme; but a shudder went through the whole of them notwithstanding. The baby, on the contrary, began to laugh and crow; while the nurse gave a start and a smothered cry, for she thought she was struck with paralysis: she could not feel the baby in her arms. But she clasped it and said nothing.

The mischief was done.

III

She Can't Be Ours

Her atrocious aunt had deprived the child of all her gravity. If you ask me how this was effected, I answer, "In the easiest way in the world. She had only to destroy gravitation." For the princess was a philosopher, and knew all the *ins* and *outs* of the laws of gravitation as well as the *ins* and *outs* of her boot-lace. And being a witch as well, she could abrogate those laws in a moment; or at least so clog their wheels and rust their bearings, that they would not work at all. But we have more to do with what followed than with how it was done.

The first awkwardness that resulted from this unhappy privation was, that the moment the nurse began to float the baby up and down, she flew from her arms towards the ceiling. Happily, the resistance of the air brought her ascending career to a close within a foot of it. There she remained, horizontal as when she left her nurse's arms, kicking and laughing amazingly. The nurse in terror flew to the bell, and begged the footman, who answered it, to bring up the house-steps directly. Trembling in every limb, she climbed upon the steps, and had to stand upon the very top, and reach up, before she could catch the floating tail of the baby's long clothes.

When the strange fact came to be known, there was a terrible commotion in the palace. The occasion of its discovery by the king was naturally a repetition of the nurse's experience. Astonished that he felt no weight when the child was laid in his arms, he began to wave her up and—not down; for she slowly ascended to the ceiling as before, and there remained floating in perfect comfort and satisfaction, as was testified by her peals of tiny laughter. The king stood staring up in speechless amazement, and trembled so that his beard shook like grass in the wind. At last, turning to the queen, who was just as horror-struck as himself, he said, gasping, staring, and stammering,—

"She *can't* be ours, queen!"

Now the queen was much cleverer than the king, and had begun already to suspect that "this effect defective came by cause."

"I am sure she is ours," answered she. "But we ought to have taken better care of her at the christening. People who were never invited ought not to have been present."

"Oh, ho!" said the king, tapping his forehead with his forefinger, "I have it all. I've found her out. Don't you see it, queen? Princess Makemnoit has bewitched her."

"That's just what I say," answered the queen.

"I beg your pardon, my love; I did not hear you.—John! bring the steps I get on my throne with."

For he was a little king with a great throne, like many other kings.

The throne-steps were brought, and set upon the dining-table, and John got upon the top of them. But he could not reach the little princess, who lay like a baby-laughter-cloud in the air, exploding continuously.

"Take the tongs, John," said his Majesty; and getting up on the table, he handed them to him.

John could reach the baby now, and the little princess was handed down by the tongs.

IV

Where Is She?

One fine summer day, a month after these her first adventures, during which time she had been very carefully

17

watched, the princess was lying on the bed in the queen's own chamber, fast asleep. One of the windows was open, for it was noon, and the day was so sultry that the little girl was wrapped in nothing less ethereal than slumber itself. The queen came into the room, and not observing that the baby was on the bed, opened another window. A frolicsome fairy wind, which had been watching for a chance of mischief, rushed in at the one window, and taking its way over the bed where the child was lying, caught her up, and rolling and floating her along like a piece of flue, or a dandelion seed, carried her with it through the opposite window, and away. The queen went down-stairs, quite ignorant of the loss she had herself occasioned.

When the nurse returned, she supposed that her Majesty had carried her off, and, dreading a scolding, delayed making inquiry about her. But hearing nothing, she grew uneasy, and went at length to the queen's boudoir, where she found her Majesty.

"Please, your Majesty, shall I take the baby?" said she.

"Where is she?" asked the queen.

"Please forgive me. I know it was wrong."

"What do you mean?" said the queen, looking grave.

"Oh! don't frighten me, your Majesty!" exclaimed the nurse, clasping her hands.

The queen saw that something was amiss, and fell down in a faint. The nurse rushed about the palace, screaming, "My baby! my baby!"

Every one ran to the queen's room. But the queen could give no orders. They soon found out, however, that the princess was missing, and in a moment the palace was like a beehive in a garden; and in one minute more the queen was brought to herself by a great shout and a clapping of hands. They had found the princess fast asleep under a rose-bush, to which the elvish little windpuff had carried her, finishing its mischief by shaking a shower of red rose-leaves all over the little white sleeper. Startled by the noise the servants made, she woke, and, furious with glee, scattered the rose-leaves in all directions, like a shower of spray in the sunset.

She was watched more carefully after this, no doubt; yet it would be endless to relate all the odd incidents resulting from this peculiarity of the young princess. But there never was a baby in a house, not to say a palace, that kept the household in such constant good humour, at least below-stairs. If it was not easy for her nurses to hold her, at least she made neither their arms nor their hearts ache. And she was so nice to play at ball with! There was positively no danger of letting her fall. They might throw her down, or knock her down, or push her down, but couldn't *let* her down. It is true, they might let her fly into the fire or the coal-hole, or through the window; but none of these accidents had happened as yet.

If you heard peals of laughter resounding from some unknown region, you might be sure enough of the cause. Going down into the kitchen, or *the room,* you would find Jane and Thomas, and Robert and Susan, all and sum, playing at ball with the little princess. She was the ball herself, and did not enjoy it the less for that. Away she went, flying from one to another, screeching with laughter. And the servants loved the ball itself better even than the game. But they had to take some care how they threw her, for if she received an upward direction, she would never come down again without being fetched.

V

What Is to Be Done?

But above-stairs it was different. One day, for instance, after breakfast, the king went into his counting-house, and counted out his money.

The operation gave him no pleasure. "To think," said

he to himself, "that every one of these gold sovereigns weighs a quarter of an ounce, and my real, live, flesh-and-blood princess weighs nothing at all!"

And he hated his gold sovereigns, as they lay with a broad smile of self-satisfaction all over their yellow faces.

The queen was in the parlour, eating bread and honey. But at the second mouthful she burst out crying, and could not swallow it. The king heard her sobbing. Glad of anybody, but especially of his queen, to quarrel with, he clashed his gold sovereigns into his money-box, clapped his crown on his head, and rushed into the parlour.

"What is all this about?" exclaimed he. "What are you crying for, queen?"

"I can't eat it," said the queen, looking ruefully at the honey-pot.

"No wonder!" retorted the king. "You've just eaten your breakfast—two turkey eggs, and three anchovies."

"Oh, that's not it!" sobbed her Majesty. "It's my child, my child!"

"Well, what's the matter with your child? She's neither up the chimney nor down the draw-well. Just hear her laughing."

Yet the king could not help a sigh, which he tried to turn into a cough, saying,—

"It is a good thing to be light-hearted, I am sure, whether she be ours or not."

"It is a bad thing to be light-headed," answered the queen, looking with prophetic soul far into the future.

"'T is a good thing to light-handed," said the king.

"'T is a bad thing to be light-fingered," answered the queen.

"'T is a good thing to be light-footed," said the king.

"'T is a bad thing—" began the queen; but the king interrupted her.

"In fact," said he, with the tone of one who concludes

an argument in which he has had only imaginary opponents, and in which, therefore, he has come off triumphant—"in fact, it is a good thing altogether to be light-bodied."

"But it is a bad thing altogether to be light-minded," retorted the queen, who was beginning to lose her temper.

This last answer quite discomfited his Majesty, who turned on his heel, and betook himself to his counting-house again. But he was not half-way towards it, when the voice of his queen overtook him.

"And it's a bad thing to be light-haired," screamed she, determined to have more last words, now that her spirit was roused.

The queen's hair was black as night; and the king's had been, and his daughter's was, golden as morning. But it was not this reflection on his hair that arrested him; it was the double use of the word *light*. For the king hated all witticisms, and punning especially. And besides, he could not tell whether the queen meant light-*haired* or light-*heired;* for why might she not aspirate her vowels when she was exasperated herself?

He turned upon his other heel, and rejoined her. She looked angry still, because she knew that she was guilty, or, what was much the same, knew that he thought so.

"My dear queen," said he, "duplicity of any sort is exceedingly objectionable between married people of any rank, not to say kings and queens; and the most objectionable form duplicity can assume is that of punning."

"There!" said the queen, "I never made a jest, but I broke it in the making. I am the most unfortunate woman in the world!"

She looked so rueful that the king took her in his arms; and they sat down to consult.

"Can you bear this?" said the king.

"No, I can't," said the queen.

"Well, what's to be done?" said the king.

"I'm sure I don't know," said the queen. "But might you not try an apology?"

"To my old sister, I suppose you mean?" said the king.

"Yes," said the queen.

"Well, I don't mind," said the king.

So he went the next morning to the house of the princess, and, making a very humble apology, begged her to undo the spell. But the princess declared, with a grave face, that she knew nothing at all about it. Her eyes, however, shone pink, which was a sign that she was happy. She advised the king and queen to have patience, and to mend their ways. The king returned disconsolate. The queen tried to comfort him.

"We will wait till she is older. She may then be able to suggest something herself. She will know at least how she feels, and explain things to us."

"But what if she should marry?" exclaimed the king, in sudden consternation at the idea.

"Well, what of that?" rejoined the queen.

"Just think! If she were to have children! In the course of a hundred years the air might be as full of floating children as of gossamers in autumn."

"That is no business of ours," replied the queen. "Besides, by that time they will have learned to take care of themselves."

A sigh was the king's only answer.

He would have consulted the court physicians; but he was afraid they would try experiments upon her.

VI

She Laughs Too Much

Meantime, notwithstanding awkward occurrences, and griefs that she brought upon her parents, the little princess laughed and grew—not fat, but plump and tall.

She reached the age of seventeen, without having fallen into any worse scrape than a chimney; by rescuing her from which, a little bird-nesting urchin got fame and a black face. Nor, thoughtless as she was, had she committed anything worse than laughter at everybody and everything that came in her way. When she was told, for the sake of experiment, that General Clanrunfort was cut to pieces with all his troops, she laughed; when she heard the enemy was on his way to besiege her papa's capital, she laughed hugely; but when she was told that the city would certainly be abandoned to the mercy of the enemy's soldiery—why, then she laughed immoderately. She never could be brought to see the serious side of anything. When her mother cried, she said,—

"What queer faces mamma makes! And she squeezes water out of her cheeks! Funny mamma!"

And when her papa stormed at her, she laughed, and danced round and round him, clapping her hands, and crying—

"Do it again, papa. Do it again! It's such fun! Dear, funny papa!"

And if he tried to catch her, she glided from him in an instant, not in the least afraid of him, but thinking it part of the game not to be caught. With one push of her foot, she would be floating in the air above his head; or she would go dancing backwards and forwards and sideways, like a great butterfly. It happened several times, when her father and mother were holding a consultation about her in private, that they were interrupted by vainly repressed outbursts of laughter over their heads; and looking up with indignation, saw her floating at full length in the air above them, whence she regarded them with the most comical appreciation of the position.

One day an awkward accident happened. The princess had come out upon the lawn with one of her attendants, who held her by the hand. Spying her father at the other side of the lawn, she snatched her hand from the maid's, and sped across to him. Now when she wanted to run alone, her custom was to catch up a stone in each hand, so that she might come down again after a bound. Whatever she wore as part of her attire had no effect in this way: even gold, when it thus became as it were a part of herself, lost all its weight for the time. But whatever she only held in her hands retained its downward tendency.

On this occasion she could see nothing to catch up but a huge toad, that was walking across the lawn as if he had a hundred years to do it in. Not knowing what disgust meant, for this was one of her peculiarities, she snatched up the toad and bounded away. She had almost reached her father, and he was holding out his arms to receive her, and take from her lips the kiss which hovered on them like a butterfly on a rosebud, when a puff of wind blew her aside into the arms of a young page, who had just been receiving a message from his Majesty.

Now it was no great peculiarity in the princess that, once she was set agoing, it always cost her time and trouble to check herself. On this occasion there was no time. She *must* kiss—and she kissed the page. She did not mind it much; for she had no shyness in her composition; and she knew, besides, that she could not help it. So she only laughed, like a musical box. The poor page fared the worst. For the princess, trying to correct the unfortunate tendency of the kiss, put out her hands to keep her off the page; so that, along with the kiss, he received, on the other cheek, a slap with the huge black toad, which she poked right into his eye. He tried to laugh, too, but the attempt resulted in such an odd contortion of countenance, as showed that there was no danger of his pluming himself on the kiss. As for the king, his dignity was greatly hurt, and he did not speak to the page for a whole month.

I may here remark that it was very amusing to see her

run, if her mode of progression could properly be called running. For first she would make a bound; then, having alighted, she would run a few steps, and make another bound. Sometimes she would fancy she had reached the ground before she actually had, and her feet would go backwards and forwards, running upon nothing at all, like those of a chicken on its back. Then she would laugh like the very spirit of fun; only in her laugh there was something missing. What it was, I find myself unable to describe. I think it was a certain tone, depending upon the possibility of sorrow—*morbidezza*, perhaps. She never smiled.

VII
Try Metaphysics

After a long avoidance of the painful subject, the king and queen resolved to hold a council of three upon it; and so they sent for the princess. In she came, sliding and flitting and gliding from one piece of furniture to another, and put herself at last in an arm-chair, in a sitting posture. Whether she could be said *to sit*, seeing she received no support from the seat of the chair, I do not pretend to determine.

"My dear child," said the king, "you must be aware by this time that you are not exactly like other people."

"Oh, you dear funny papa! I have got a nose, and two eyes, and all the rest. So have you. So has mamma."

"Now be serious, my dear, for once," said the queen.

"No, thank you, mamma; I had rather not."

"Would you not like to be able to walk like other people?" said the king.

"No indeed, I should think not. You only crawl. You are such slow coaches!"

"How do you feel, my child?" he resumed, after a pause of discomfiture.

"Quite well, thank you."

"I mean, what do you feel like?"

"Like nothing at all, that I know of."

"You must feel like something."

"I feel like a princess with such a funny papa, and such a dear pet of a queen-mamma!"

"Now really!" began the queen; but the princess interrupted her.

"Oh, yes," she added, "I remember. I have a curious feeling sometimes, as if I were the only person that had any sense in the whole world."

She had been trying to behave herself with dignity; but now she burst into a violent fit of laughter, threw herself backwards over the chair, and went rolling about the floor in an ecstasy of enjoyment. The king picked her up easier than one does a down quilt, and replaced her in her former relation to the chair. The exact preposition expressing this relation I do not happen to know.

"Is there nothing you wish for?" resumed the king, who had learned by this time that it was useless to be angry with her.

"Oh, you dear papa!—yes," answered she.

"What is it, my darling?"

"I have been longing for it—oh, such a time!—ever since last night."

"Tell me what it is."

"Will you promise to let me have it?"

The king was on the point of saying *Yes*, but the wiser queen checked him with a single motion of her head.

"Tell me what it is first," said he.

"No no. Promise first."

"I dare not. What is it?"

"Mind, I hold you to your promise.—It is—to be tied to the end of a string—a very long string indeed, and be flown like a kite. Oh, such fun! I would rain rose-water, and hail sugar-plums, and snow whipped-cream, and—and—and—"

A fit of laughing checked her; and she would have been off again over the floor, had not the king started up and caught her just in time. Seeing that nothing but talk could be got out of her, he range the bell, and sent her away with two of her ladies-in-waiting.

"Now, queen," he said, turning to her Majesty, "what *is* to be done?"

"There is but one thing left," answered she. "Let us consult the college of Metaphysicians."

"Bravo!" cried the king; "we will."

Now at the head of this college were two very wise Chinese philosophers—by name Hum-Drum and Kopy-Keck. For them the king sent; and straightway they came. In a long speech he communicated to them what they knew very well already—as who did not?—namely, the peculiar condition of his daughter in relation to the globe on which she dwelt; and requested them to consult together as to what might be the cause and probable cure of her *infirmity*. The king laid stress upon the word, but failed to discover his own pun. The queen laughed; but Hum-Drum and Kopy-Keck heard with humility and retired in silence.

Their consultation consisted chiefly in propounding and supporting, for the thousandth time, each his favourite theories. For the condition of the princess afforded delightful scope for the discussion of every question arising from the division of thought—in fact, of all the Metaphysics of the Chinese Empire. But it is only justice to say that they did not altogether neglect the discussion of the practical question, *what was to be done*.

Hum-Drum was a Materialist, and Kopy-Keck was a Spiritualist. The former was slow and sententious; the latter was quick and flighty: the latter had generally the first word; the former the last.

"I reassert my former assertion," began Kopy-Keck, with a plunge. "There is not a fault in the princess, body or soul; only they are wrong put together. Listen to me

27

now, Hum-Drum, and I will tell you in brief what I think. Don't speak. Don't answer me. I *won't* hear you till I have done.—At that decisive moment, when souls seek their appointed habitations, two eager souls met, struck, rebounded, lost their way, and arrived each at the wrong place. The soul of the princess was one of those, and she went far astray. She does not belong by rights to this world at all, but to some other planet, probably Mercury. Her proclivity to her true sphere destroys all the natural influence which this orb would otherwise possess over her corporeal frame. She cares for nothing here. There is no relation between her and this world.

"She must therefore be taught, by the sternest compulsion, to take an interest in the earth as the earth. She must study every department of its history—its animal history; its vegetable history; its mineral history; its social history; its moral history; its political history; its scientific history; its literary history; its musical history; its artistical history; above all, its metaphysical history. She must begin with the Chinese dynasty and end with Japan. But first of all she must study geology, and especially the history of the extinct races of animals—their natures, their habits, their loves, their hates, their revenges. She must——"

"Hold, h-o-o-old!" roared Hum-Drum. "It is certainly my turn now. My rooted and insubvertible conviction is that the causes of the anomalies evident in the princess's condition are strictly and solely physical. But that is only tantamount to acknowledging that they exist. Hear my opinion.—From some cause or other, of no importance to our inquiry, the motion of her heart has been reversed. That remarkable combination of the suction and the force-pump works the wrong way—I mean in the case of the unfortunate princess, it draws in where it should force out, and forces out where it should draw in. The offices of the auricles and the ventricles are subverted. The blood is sent forth by the veins, and returns by the arteries. Consequently it is running the wrong way through all her corporeal organism—lungs and all. Is it then at all mysterious, seeing that such is the case, that on the other particular of gravitation as well, she should differ from normal humanity? My proposal for the cure is this:—

"Phlebotomize until she is reduced to the last point of safety. Let it be effected, if necessary, in a warm bath. When she is reduced to a state of perfect asphyxy, apply a ligature to the left ankle, drawing it as tight as the bone will bear. Apply, at the same moment, another of equal tension around the right wrist. By means of plates constructed for the purpose, place the other foot and hand under the receivers of two air-pumps. Exhaust the receivers. Exhibit a pint of French brandy, and await the result."

"Which would presently arrive in the form of grim Death," said Kopy-Keck.

"If it should, she would yet die in doing our duty," retorted Hum-Drum.

But their Majesties had too much tenderness for their volatile offspring to subject her to either of the schemes of the equally unscrupulous philosophers. Indeed, the most complete knowledge of the laws of nature would have been unserviceable in her case; for it was impossible to classify her. She was a fifth imponderable body, sharing all the other properties of the ponderable.

VIII
Try a Drop of Water

Perhaps the best thing for the princess would have been to fall in love. But how a princess who had no gravity could fall into anything is a difficulty—perhaps *the* difficulty. As for her own feelings on the subject, she did not even know that there was such a beehive of honey and stings to be fallen into. But now I come to mention another curious fact about her.

The palace was built on the shores of the loveliest lake in the world; and the princess loved this lake more than father or mother. The root of this preference no doubt, although the princess did not recognize it as such, was, that the moment she got into it, she recovered the natural right of which she had been so wickedly deprived—namely, gravity. Whether this was owing to the fact that water had been employed as the means of conveying the injury, I do not know. But it is certain that she could swim and dive like the duck that her old nurse said she was. The manner in which this alleviation of her misfortune was discovered was as follows.

One summer evening, during the carnival of the country, she had been taken upon the lake by the king and queen in the royal barge. They were accompanied by many of the courtiers in a fleet of little boats. In the middle of the lake she wanted to get into the lord chancellor's barge, for his daughter, who was a great favourite with her, was in it with her father.

Now though the old king rarely condescended to make light of his misfortune, yet, happening on this occasion to be in a particularly good humour, as the barges approached each other, he caught up the princess to throw her into the chancellor's barge. He lost his balance, however, and, dropping into the bottom of the barge lost his hold of his daughter; not, however, before imparting to her the downward tendency of his own person, though in a somewhat different direction; for, as the king fell into the boat, she fell into the water. With a burst of delighted laughter she disappeared into the lake. A cry of horror ascended from the boats. They had never seen the princess go down before. Half the men were under water in a moment; but they had all, one after another come up to the surface again for breath, when—tinkle, tinkle, babble, and gush! came the princess's laugh over the water from far away. There she was, swimming like a swan. Nor would she come out for king or queen, chancellor or daughter. She was perfectly obstinate.

But at the same time she seemed more sedate than usual. Perhaps that was because a great pleasure spoils laughing. At all events, after this, the passion of her life was to get into the water, and she was always the better behaved and the more beautiful the more she had of it. Summer and winter it was quite the same; only she could not stay so long in the water when they had to break the ice to let her in. Any day, from morning to evening in summer, she might be descried—a streak of white in the blue water—lying as still as the shadow of a cloud, or shooting along like a dolphin; disappearing, and coming up again far off, just where one did not expect her.

She would have been in the lake of a night too, if she could have had her way; for the balcony of her window overhung a deep pool in it; and through a shallow reedy passage she could have swum out into the wide wet water, and no one would have been any the wiser. Indeed, when she happened to wake in the moonlight she could hardly resist the temptation. But there was the sad difficulty of getting into it. She had as great a dread of the air as some children have of the water. For the slightest gust of wind would blow her away; and a gust might arise in the stillest moment. And if she gave herself a push towards the water and just failed of reaching it, her situation would be dreadfully awkward, irrespective of the wind; for at best there she would have to remain, suspended in her night-gown, till she was seen and angled for by somebody from the window.

"Oh! if I had my gravity," thought she, contemplating the water, "I would flash off this balcony like a long

white sea-bird, headlong into the darling wetness. Heigh-
ho!''

This was the only consideration that made her wish to
be like other people.

Another reason for her being fond of the water was
that in it alone she enjoyed any freedom. For she could
not walk out without a *cortége*, consisting in part of a
troop of light-horse, for fear of the liberties which the
wind might take with her. And the king grew more apprehensive with increasing years, till at last he would not
allow her to walk abroad at all without some twenty
silken cords fastened to as many parts of her dress, and
held by twenty noblemen. Of course horseback was out
of the question. But she bade good-bye to all this ceremony when she got into the water.

And so remarkable were its effects upon her, especially in restoring her for the time to the ordinary human gravity, that Hum-Drum and Kopy-Keck agreed in
recommending the king to bury her alive for three years;
in the hope that, as the water did her so much good, the
earth would do her yet more. But the king had some vul-
gar prejudices against the experiment, and would not
give his consent. Foiled in this, they yet agreed in another recommendation; which, seeing that one imported
his opinions from China and the other from Tibet, was
very remarkable indeed. They argued that, if water of
external origin and application could be so efficacious,
water from a deeper source might work a perfect cure; in
short, that if the poor afflicted princess could by any
means be made to cry, she might recover her lost gravity.

But how was this to be brought about? Therein lay all
the difficulty—to meet which the philosophers were not
wise enough. To make the princess cry was as impossible as to make her weigh. They sent for a professional
beggar; commanded him to prepare his most touching
oracle of woe; helped him out of the court charade box,

to whatever he wanted for dressing up, and promised great rewards in the event of his success. But it was all in vain. She listened to the mendicant artist's story, and gazed at his marvellous make up, till she could contain herself no longer, and went into the most undignified contortions for relief, shrieking, positively screeching with laughter.

When she had a little recovered herself, she ordered her attendants to drive him away, and not give him a single copper; whereupon his look of mortified discomfiture wrought her punishment and his revenge, for it sent her into violent hysterics, from which she was with difficulty recovered.

But so anxious was the king that the suggestion should have a fair trial, that he put himself in a rage one day, and, rushing up to her room, gave her an awful whipping. Yet not a tear would flow. She looked grave, and her laughing sounded uncommonly like screaming—that was all. The good old tyrant, though he put on his best gold spectacles to look, could not discover the smallest cloud in the serene blue of her eyes.

IX

Put Me in Again

It must have been about this time that the son of a king, who lived a thousand miles from Lagobel, set out to look for the daughter of a queen. He travelled far and wide, but as sure as he found a princess, he found some fault in her. Of course he could not marry a mere woman, however beautiful; and there was no princess to be found worthy of him. Whether the prince was so near perfection that he had a right to demand perfection itself, I cannot pretend to say. All I know is, that he was a fine, handsome, brave, generous, well-bred, and well-behaved youth, as all princes are.

In his wanderings he had come across some reports about our princess; but as everybody said she was bewitched, he never dreamed that she could bewitch him. For what indeed could a prince do with a princess that had lost her gravity? Who could tell what she might not lose next? She might lose her visibility, or her tangibility; or, in short, the power of making impressions upon the radical sensorium; so that he should never be able to tell whether she was dead or alive. Of course, he made no further inquiries about her.

One day he lost sight of his retinue in a great forest. These forests are very useful in delivering princes from their courtiers, like a sieve that keeps back the bran. Then the princes get away to follow their fortunes. In this they have the advantage of the princesses, who are forced to marry before they have had a bit of fun. I wish our princesses got lost in a forest sometimes.

One lovely evening, after wandering about for many days, he found that he was approaching the outskirts of this forest; for the trees had got so thin that he could see the sunset through them; and he soon came upon a kind of heath. Next he came upon signs of human neighbourhood; but by this time it was getting late, and there was nobody in the fields to direct him.

After travelling for another hour, his horse, quite worn out with long labour and lack of food, fell, and was unable to rise again. So he continued his journey on foot. At length he entered another wood—not a wild forest, but a civilized wood, through which a footpath led him to the side of a lake. Along this path the prince pursued his way through the gathering darkness. Suddenly he paused, and listened. Strange sounds came across the water. It was, in fact, the princess laughing. Now there was something odd in her laugh, as I have already hinted; for the hatching of a real hearty laugh requires the incubation of gravity; and perhaps this was how the prince mistook the laughter for screaming. Looking over the lake, he saw something white in the water; and, in an instant, he had torn off his tunic, kicked off his sandals, and plunged in. He soon reached the white object, and found that it was a woman. There was not light enough to show that she was a princess, but quite enough to show that she was a lady, for it does not want much light to see that.

Now I cannot tell how it came about,—whether she pretended to be drowning, or whether he frightened her, or caught her so as to embarrass her,—but certainly he brought her to shore in a fashion ignominious to a swimmer, and more nearly drowned than she had ever expected to be; for the water had got into her throat as often as she had tried to speak.

At the place to which he bore her, the bank was only a foot or two above the water; so he gave her a strong lift out of the water, to lay her on the bank. But, her gravitation ceasing the moment she left the water, away she went up into the air, scolding and screaming.

"You naughty, *naughty*, NAUGHTY, NAUGHTY man!" she cried.

No one had ever succeeded in putting her into a passion before. When the prince saw her ascend, he thought he must have been bewitched, and have mistaken a great swan for a lady. But the princess caught hold of the topmost cone upon a lofty fir. This came off; but she caught at another; and, in fact, stopped herself by gathering cones, dropping them as the stalks gave way. The prince, meantime, stood in the water, staring, and forgetting to get out. But the princess disappearing, he scrambled on shore, and went in the direction of the tree. There he found her climbing down one of the branches towards the stem. But in the darkness of the wood, the prince

continued in some bewilderment as to what the phenom-
enon could be; until reaching the ground, and seeing him
standing there, she caught hold of him, and said,—

"I'll tell papa."

"Oh no, you won't!" returned the prince.

"Yes, I will," she persisted. "What business had you to
pull me down out of the water, and throw me to the bottom of the air? I never did you any harm."

"Pardon me. I did not mean to hurt you."

"I don't believe you have any brains; and that is a
worse loss than your wretched gravity. I pity you."

The prince now saw that he had come upon the bewitched princess, and had already offended her. But before he could think what to say next, she burst out
angrily, giving a stamp with her foot that would have
sent her aloft again but for the hold she had of his arm,—

"Put me up directly."

"Put you up where, you beauty?" asked the prince.

He had fallen in love with her almost, already; for her
anger made her more charming than any one else had
ever beheld her; and, as far as he could see, which certainly was not far, she had not a single fault about her,
except, of course, that she had not any gravity. No prince,
however, would judge of a princess by weight. The loveliness of her foot he would hardly estimate by the depth of
the impression it could make in mud.

"Put you up where, you beauty?" asked the prince.

"In the water, you stupid!" answered the princess.

"Come, then," said the prince.

The condition of her dress, increasing her usual difficulty in walking, compelled her to cling to him; and he
could hardly persuade himself that he was not in a delightful dream, notwithstanding the torrent of musical
abuse with which she overwhelmed him. The prince being therefore in no hurry, they came upon the lake at
quite another part, where the bank was twenty-five feet

high at least; and when they had reached the edge, he turned towards the princess, and said,—

"How am I to put you in?"

"That is your business," she answered, quite snappishly. "You took me out—put me in again."

"Very well," said the prince; and, catching her up in his arms, he sprang with her from the rock. The princess had just time to give one delighted shriek of laughter before the water closed over them. When they came to the surface, she found that, for a moment or two, she could not even laugh, for she had gone down with such a rush, that it was with difficulty she recovered her breath. The instant they reached the surface—

"How do you like falling in?" said the prince.

After some effort the princess panted out,—

"Is that what you call *falling in?*"

"Yes," answered the prince, "I should think it a very tolerable specimen."

"It seemed to me like going up," rejoined she.

"My feeling was certainly one of elevation too," the prince conceded.

The princess did not appear to understand him, for she retorted his question:—

"How do *you* like falling in?" said the princess.

"Beyond everything," answered he; "for I have fallen in with the only perfect creature I ever saw."

"No more of that: I am tired of it," said the princess. Perhaps she shared her father's aversion to punning.

"Don't you like falling in, then?" said the prince.

"It is the most delightful fun I ever had in my life," answered she. "I never fell before. I wish I could learn. To think I am the only person in my father's kingdom that can't fall!"

Here the poor princess looked almost sad.

"I shall be most happy to fall in with you any time you like," said the prince, devotedly.

37

"Thank you. I don't know. Perhaps it would not be proper. But I don't care. At all events, as we have fallen in, let us have a swim together."

"With all my heart," responded the prince.

And away they went, swimming, and diving, and floating, until at last they heard cries along the shore, and saw lights glancing in all directions. It was now quite late, and there was no moon.

"I must go home," said the princess. "I am very sorry, for this is delightful."

"So am I," returned the prince. "But I am glad I haven't a home to go to—at least, I don't exactly know where it is."

"I wish I hadn't one either," rejoined the princess; "it is so stupid! I have a great mind," she continued, "to play them all a trick. Why couldn't they leave me alone? They won't trust me in the lake for a single night!—You see where that green light is burning? That is the window of my room. Now if you would just swim there with me very quietly, and when we are all but under the balcony, give me such a push—*up* you call it—as you did a little while ago, I should be able to catch hold of the balcony, and get in at the window; and then they may look for me till to-morrow morning!"

"With more obedience than pleasure," said the prince, gallantly; and away they swam, very gently.

"Will you be in the lake to-morrow night?" the prince ventured to ask.

"To be sure I will. I don't think so. Perhaps," was the princess's somewhat strange answer.

But the prince was intelligent enough not to press her further; and merely whispered, as he gave her the parting lift, "Don't tell." The only answer the princess returned was a roguish look. She was already a yard above his head. The look seemed to say, "Never fear. It is too good fun to spoil that way."

So perfectly like other people had she been in the water, that even yet the prince could scarcely believe his eyes when he saw her ascend slowly, grasp the balcony, and disappear through the window. He turned, almost expecting to see her still by his side. But he was alone in the water. So he swam away quietly, and watched the lights roving about the shore for hours after the princess was safe in her chamber. As soon as they disappeared, he landed in search of his tunic and sword, and, after some trouble, found them again. Then he made the best of his way round the lake to the other side. There the wood was wilder, and the shore steeper—rising more immediately towards the mountains which surrounded the lake on all sides, and kept sending it messages of silvery streams from morning to night, and all night long. He soon found a spot where he could see the green light in the princess's room, and where, even in the broad daylight, he would be in no danger of being discovered from the opposite shore. It was a sort of cave in the rock, where he provided himself a bed of withered leaves, and lay down too tired for hunger to keep him awake. All night long he dreamed that he was swimming with the princess.

X
Look at the Moon

Early the next morning the prince set out to look for something to eat, which he soon found at a forester's hut, where for many following days he was supplied with all that a brave prince could consider necessary. And having plenty to keep him alive for the present, he would not think of wants not yet in existence. Whenever Care intruded, this prince always bowed him out in the most princely manner.

When he returned from his breakfast to his watch cave, he saw the princess already floating about in the lake, attended by the king and queen—whom he knew by their crowns—and a great company in lovely little boats, with canopies of all the colours of the rainbow, and flags and streamers of a great many more. It was a very bright day, and soon the prince, burned up with the heat, began to long for the cold water and the cool princess. But he had to endure till twilight; for the boats had provisions on board, and it was not till the sun went down that the gay party began to vanish. Boat after boat drew away to the shore, following that of the king and queen, till only one, apparently the princess's own boat, remained. But she did not want to go home even yet, and the prince thought he saw her order the boat to the shore without her. At all events, it rowed away; and now, of all the radiant company, only one white speck remained. Then the prince began to sing.

And this is what he sung:—

> "Lady fair,
> Swan-white,
> Lift thine eyes,
> Banish night
> By the might
> Of thine eyes.

> "Snowy arms,
> Oars of snow,
> Oar her hither,
> Plashing low.
> Soft and slow,
> Oar her hither.

> "Stream behind her
> O'er the lake,
> Radiant whiteness!
> In her wake
> Following, following for her sake,
> Radiant whiteness!

"Cling about her,
Waters blue;
Part not from her,
But renew
Cold and true
Kisses round her.

"Lap me round,
Waters sad
That have left her
Make me glad,
For ye had
Kissed her ere ye left her."

Before he had finished his song, the princess was just under the place where he sat, and looking up to find him. Her ears had led her truly.

"Would you like a fall, princess?" said the prince, looking down.

"Ah! there you are! Yes, if you please, prince," said the princess, looking up.

"How do you know I am a prince, princess?" said the prince.

"Because you are a very nice young man, prince," said the princess.

"Come up then, princess."

"Fetch me, prince."

The prince took off his scarf, then his swordbelt, then his tunic, and tied them all together, and let them down. But the line was far too short. He unwound his turban, and added it to the rest, when it was all but long enough; and his purse completed it. The princess just managed to lay hold of the knot of money, and was beside him in a moment. This rock was much higher than the other, and the splash and the dive were tremendous. The princess was in ecstasies of delight, and their swim was delicious.

Night after night they met, and swam about in the dark clear lake; where such was the prince's gladness, that (whether the princess's way of looking at things infected him, or he was actually getting light-headed) he often fancied that he was swimming in the sky instead of the lake. But when he talked about being in heaven, the princess laughed at him dreadfully.

When the moon came, she brought them fresh pleasure. Everything looked strange and new in her light, with an old, withered, yet unfading newness. When the moon was nearly full, one of their great delights was to dive deep in the water, and then, turning round, look up through it at the great blot of light close above them, shimmering and trembling and wavering, spreading and contracting, seeming to melt away, and again grow solid. Then they would shoot up through the blot; and lo! there was the moon, far off, clear and steady and cold, and very lovely, at the bottom of a deeper and bluer lake than theirs, as the princess said.

The prince soon found out that while in the water the princess was very like other people. And besides this, she was not so forward in her questions or pert in her replies at sea as on shore. Neither did she laugh so much; and when she did laugh, it was more gently. She seemed altogether more modest and maidenly in the water than out of it. But when the prince, who had really fallen in love when he fell in the lake, began to talk to her about love, she always turned her head towards him and laughed. After a while she began to look puzzled, as if she were trying to understand what he meant, but could not—revealing a notion that he meant something. But as soon as ever she left the lake, she was so altered, that the prince said to himself, "If I marry her, I see no help for it: we must turn merman and mermaid, and go out to sea at once."

XI
Hiss!

The princess's pleasure in the lake had grown to a passion, and she could scarcely bear to be out of it for an hour. Imagine then her consternation, when, diving with the prince one night, a sudden suspicion seized her that the lake was not so deep as it used to be. The prince could not imagine what had happened. She shot to the surface, and, without a word, swam at full speed towards the higher side of the lake. He followed, begging to know if she was ill, or what was the matter. She never turned her head, or took the smallest notice of his question. Arrived at the shore, she coasted the rocks with minute inspection. But she was not able to come to a conclusion, for the moon was very small, and so she could not see well. She turned therefore and swam home, without saying a word to explain her conduct to the prince, of whose presence she seemed no longer conscious. He withdrew to his cave, in great perplexity and distress.

Next day she made many observations, which, alas! strengthened her fears. She saw that the banks were too dry; and that the grass on the shore, and the trailing plants on the rocks, were withering away. She caused marks to be made along the borders, and examined them, day after day, in all directions of the wind; till at last the horrible idea became a certain fact—that the surface of the lake was slowly sinking.

The poor princess nearly went out of the little mind she had. It was awful to her to see the lake, which she loved more than any living thing, lie dying before her eyes. It sank away, slowly vanishing. The tops of rocks that had never been seen till now, began to appear far down in the clear water. Before long they were dry in the sun. It was fearful to think of the mud that would soon lie there baking and festering full of lovely creatures dying, and ugly creatures coming to life, like the unmaking of a world. And how hot the sun would be without any lake! She could not bear to swim in it any more, and began to pine away. Her life seemed bound up with it; and ever as the lake sank, she pined. People said she would not live an hour after the lake was gone.

But she never cried.

Proclamation was made to all the kingdom, that whosoever should discover the cause of the lake's decrease, would be rewarded after a princely fashion. Hum-Drum and Kopy-Keck applied themselves to their physics and metaphysics; but in vain. Not even they could suggest a cause.

Now the fact was that the old princess was at the root of the mischief. When she heard that her niece found more pleasure in the water than any one else had out of it, she went into a rage, and cursed herself for her want of foresight.

"But," said she, "I will soon set all right. The king and the people shall die of thirst; their brains shall boil and frizzle in their skulls before I will lose my revenge."

And she laughed a ferocious laugh, that made the hairs on the back of her black cat stand erect with terror.

Then she went to an old chest in the room, and opening it, took out what looked like a piece of dried seaweed. This she threw into a tub of water. Then she threw some powder into the water, and stirred it with her bare arm, muttering over it words of hideous sound, and yet more hideous import. Then she set the tub aside, and took from the chest a huge bunch of a hundred rusty keys, that clattered in her shaking hands. Then she sat down and proceeded to oil them all.

Before she had finished, out from the tub, the water of

which had kept on a slow motion ever since she had ceased stirring it, came the head and half the body of a huge gray snake. But the witch did not look round. It grew out of the tub, waving itself backwards and forwards with a slow horizontal motion, till it reached the princess, when it laid its head upon her shoulder, and gave a low hiss in her ear. She started—but with joy; and seeing the head resting on her shoulder, drew it towards her and kissed it. Then she drew it all out of the tub, and wound it round her body. It was one of those dreadful creatures which few have ever beheld—the White Snakes of Darkness.

Then she took the keys and went down to her cellar; and as she unlocked the door she said to herself,—

"This *is* worth living for!"

Locking the door behind her, she descended a few steps into the cellar, and crossing it, unlocked another door into a dark, narrow passage. She locked this also behind her, and descended a few more steps. If any one had followed the witch-princess, he would have heard her unlock exactly one hundred doors, and descend a few steps after unlocking each. When she had unlocked the last, she entered a vast cave, the roof of which was supported by huge natural pillars of rock. Now this roof was the under side of the bottom of the lake.

She then untwined the snake from her body, and held it by the tail high above her. The hideous creature stretched up its head towards the roof of the cavern, which it was just able to reach. It then began to move its head backwards and forwards, with a slow oscillating motion, as if looking for something. At the same moment the witch began to walk round and round the cavern, coming nearer to the centre every circuit; while the head of the snake described the same path over the roof that she did over the floor, for she kept holding it up. And still it kept slowly oscillating. Round and round the cavern they went, ever lessening the circuit, till at last the snake made a sudden dart, and clung to the roof with its mouth.

"That's right, my beauty!" cried the princess; "drain it dry."

She let it go, left it hanging, and sat down on a great stone, with her black cat, which had followed her all round the cave, by her side. Then she began to knit and mutter awful words. The snake hung like a huge leech, sucking at the stone; the cat stood with his back arched, and his tail like a piece of cable, looking up at the snake; and the old woman sat and knitted and muttered.

Seven days and seven nights they remained thus; when suddenly the serpent dropped from the roof as if exhausted and shrivelled up till it was again like a piece of dried seaweed. The witch started to her feet, picked it up, put it in her pocket, and looked up at the roof. One drop of water was trembling on the spot where the snake had been sucking. As soon as she saw that, she turned and fled, followed by her cat. Shutting the door in a terrible hurry, she locked it, and having muttered some frightful words, sped to the next, which also she locked and muttered over; and so with all the hundred doors, till she arrived in her own cellar. Then she sat down on the floor ready to faint, but listening with malicious delight to the rushing of the water, which she could hear distinctly through all the hundred doors.

But this was not enough. Now that she had tasted revenge, she lost her patience. Without further measures, the lake would be too long in disappearing. So the next night, with the last shred of the dying old moon rising, she took some of the water in which she had revived the snake, put it in a bottle, and set out, accompanied by her cat. Before morning she had made the entire circuit of the lake, muttering fearful words as she crossed every stream, and casting into it some of the water out of her bottle.

When she had finished the circuit she muttered yet again, and flung a handful of water towards the moon. Thereupon every spring in the country ceased to throb and bubble, dying away like the pulse of a dying man. The next day there was no sound of falling water to be heard along the borders of the lake. The very courses were dry; and the mountains showed no silvery streaks down their dark sides. And not alone had the fountains of mother Earth ceased to flow; for all the babies throughout the country were crying dreadfully—only without tears.

XII

Where Is the Prince?

Never since the night when the princess left him so abruptly had the prince had a single interview with her. He had seen her once or twice in the lake; but as far as he could discover, she had not been in it any more at night. He had sat and sung, and looked in vain for his Nereid; while she, like a true Nereid, was wasting away with her lake, sinking as it sank, withering as it dried. When at length he discovered the change that was taking place in the level of the water, he was in great alarm and perplexity. He could not tell whether the lake was dying because the lady had forsaken it; or whether the lady would not come because the lake had begun to sink. But he resolved to know so much at least.

He disguised himself, and, going to the palace, requested to see the lord chamberlain. His appearance at once gained his request; and the lord chamberlain, being a man of some insight, perceived that there was more in the prince's solicitation than met the ear. He felt likewise that no one could tell whence a solution of the present difficulties might arise. So he granted the prince's prayer to be made shoeblack to the princess. It was rather cunning in the prince to request such an easy post, for the princess could not possibly soil as many shoes as other princesses.

He soon learned all that could be told about the princess. He went nearly distracted; but after roaming about the lake for days, and diving in every depth that remained, all that he could do was to put an extra polish on the dainty pair of boots that was never called for.

For the princess kept her room, with the curtains drawn to shut out the dying lake. But could not shut it out of her mind for a moment. It haunted her imagination so that she felt as if the lake were her soul, drying up within her, first to mud, then to madness and death. She thus brooded over the change, with all its dreadful accompaniments, till she was nearly distracted. As for the prince, she had forgotten him. However much she had enjoyed his company in the water, she did not care for him without it. But she seemed to have forgotten her father and mother too.

The lake went on sinking. Small slimy spots began to appear, which glittered steadily amidst the changeful shine of the water. These grew to broad patches of mud, which widened and spread, with rocks here and there, and floundering fishes and crawling eels swarming. The people went everywhere catching these, and looking for anything that might have dropped from the royal boats.

At length the lake was all but gone, only a few of the deepest pools remaining unexhausted.

It happened one day that a party of youngsters found themselves on the brink of one of these pools in the very centre of the lake. It was a rocky basin of considerable depth. Looking in, they saw at the bottom something that shone yellow in the sun. A little boy jumped in and dived for it. It was a plate of gold covered with writing. They carried it to the king.

On one side of it stood these words:—

> "Death alone from death can save.
> Love is death, and so is brave
> Love can fill the deepest grave.
> Love loves on beneath the wave."

Now this was enigmatical enough to the king and courtiers. But the reverse of the plate explained it a little. Its writing amounted to this:—

"If the lake should disappear, they must find the hole through which the water ran. But it would be useless to try to stop it by any ordinary means. There was but one effectual mode. The body of a living man could alone stanch the flow. The man must give himself of his own will; and the lake must take his life as it filled. Otherwise the offering would be of no avail. If the nation could not provide one hero, it was time it should perish."

XIII

Here I Am

This was a very disheartening revelation to the king— not that he was unwilling to sacrifice a subject, but that he was hopeless of finding a man willing to sacrifice himself. No time was to be lost, however, for the princess was lying motionless on her bed, and taking no nourishment but lake-water, which was now none of the best. Therefore the king caused the contents of the wonderful plate of gold to be published throughout the country.

No one, however, came forward.

The prince, having gone several days' journey into the forest, to consult a hermit whom he had met there on his way to Lagobel, knew nothing of the oracle till his return.

When he had acquainted himself with all the particulars, he sat down and thought,—

"She will die if I don't do it, and life would be nothing to me without her; so I shall lose nothing by doing it. And life will be as pleasant to her as ever, for she will soon forget me. And there will be so much more beauty and happiness in the world!—To be sure, I shall not see it." (Here the poor prince gave a sigh.) "How lovely the lake will be in the moonlight, with that glorious creature sporting in it like a wild goddess!—It is rather hard to be drowned by inches, though. Let me see—that will be seventy inches of me to drown." (Here he tried to laugh, but could not.) "The longer the better, however," he resumed; "for can I not bargain that the princess shall be beside me all the time? So I shall see her once more, kiss her perhaps,—who knows? and die looking in her eyes. It will be no death. At least, I shall not feel it. And to see the lake filling for the beauty again!—All right! I am ready."

He kissed the princess's boot, laid it down, and hurried to the king's apartment. But feeling, as he went, that anything sentimental would be disagreeable, he resolved to carry off the whole affair with nonchalance. So he knocked at the door of the king's counting-house, where it was all but a capital crime to disturb him.

When the king heard the knock he started up, and opened the door in a rage. Seeing only the shoeblack, he drew his sword. This, I am sorry to say, was his usual mode of asserting his regality when he thought his dignity was in danger. But the prince was not in the least alarmed.

"Please your majesty, I'm your butler," said he.

"My butler! you lying rascal! What do you mean."

"I mean, I will cork your big bottle."

"Is the fellow mad?" bawled the king, raising the point of his sword.

"I will put the stopper—plug—what you call it, in your leaky lake, grand monarch," said the prince.

The king was in such a rage that before he could speak he had time to cool, and to reflect that it would be great waste to kill the only man who was willing to be useful in the present emergency, seeing that in the end the insolent fellow would be as dead as if he had died by his majesty's own hand.

"Oh!" said he at last, putting up his sword with difficulty, it was so long; "I am obliged to you, you young fool! Take a glass of wine?"

"No, thank you," replied the prince.

"Very well," said the king. "Would you like to run and see your parents before you make your experiment?"

"No, thank you," said the prince.

"Then we will go and look for the hole at once," said his majesty, and proceeded to call some attendants.

"Stop, please your majesty; I have a condition to make," interposed the prince.

"What!" exclaimed the king, "a condition! and with me! How dare you?"

"As you please," returned the prince, coolly. "I wish your majesty a good morning."

"You wretch! I will have you put in a sack, and stuck in the hole."

"Very well, your majesty," replied the prince, becoming a little more respectful, lest the wrath of the king should deprive him of the pleasure of dying for the princess. "But what good will that do your majesty? Please to remember that the oracle says the victim must offer himself."

"Well, you *have* offered yourself," retorted the king.

"Yes, upon one condition."

"Condition again!" roared the king, once more drawing his sword. "Begone! Somebody else will be glad enough to take the honour off your shoulders."

"Your majesty knows it will not be easy to get another to take my place."

"Well, what is your condition?" growled the king, feeling that the prince was right.

"Only this," replied the prince; "that, as I must on no account die before I am fairly drowned, and the waiting will be rather wearisome, the princess, your daughter, shall go with me, feed me with her own hands, and look at me now and then to comfort me; for you must confess it *is* rather hard. As soon as the water is up to my eyes, she may go and be happy, and forget her poor shoeblack."

Here the prince's voice faltered, and he very nearly grew sentimental, in spite of his resolution.

"Why didn't you tell me before what your condition was? Such a fuss about nothing!" exclaimed the king.

"Do you grant it?" persisted the prince.

"Of course I do," replied the king.

"Very well. I am ready."

"Go and have some dinner, then, while I set my people to find the place."

The king ordered out his guards, and gave directions to the officers to find the hole in the lake at once. So the bed of the lake was marked out in divisions and thoroughly examined, and in an hour or so the hole was discovered. It was in the middle of a stone, near the centre of the lake, in the very pool where the golden plate had been found. It was a three-cornered hole of no great size. There was water all round the stone, but very little was flowing through the hole.

XIV

This Is Very Kind of You

The prince went to dress for the occasion, for he was resolved to die like a prince.

When the princess heard that a man had offered to die for her, she was so transported that she jumped off the bed, feeble as she was, and danced about the room for joy. She did not care who the man was; that was nothing to her. The hole wanted stopping; and if only a man would do, why, take one. In an hour or two more everything was ready. Her maid dressed her in haste, and they carried her to the side of the lake. When she saw it she shrieked, and covered her face with her hands. They bore her across to the stone, where they had already placed a little boat for her. The water was not deep enough to float it, but they hoped it would be, before long. They laid her on cushions, placed in the boat wines and fruits and other nice things, and stretched a canopy over all.

In a few minutes the prince appeared. The princess recognized him at once, but did not think it worth while to acknowledge him.

"Here I am," said the prince. "Put me in."

"They told me it was a shoeblack," said the princess.

"So I am," said the prince. "I blacked your little boots three times a day, because they were all I could get of you. Put me in."

The courtiers did not resent his bluntness, except by saying to each other that he was taking it out in impudence.

But how was he to be put in? The golden plate contained no instructions on this point. The prince looked at the hole, and saw but one way. He put both his legs into it, sitting on the stone, and, stooping forward, covered the corner that remained open with his two hands. In this uncomfortable position he resolved to abide his fate, and turning to the people, said,—

"Now you can go."

The king had already gone home to dinner.

"Now you can go," repeated the princess after him, like a parrot.

The people obeyed her and went.

Presently a little wave flowed over the stone, and wetted one of the prince's knees. But he did not mind it much. He began to sing, and the song he sang was this:—

> "As a world that has no well,
> Darkly bright in forest dell;
> As a world without the gleam
> Of the downward-going stream;
> As a world without the glance
> Of the ocean's fair expanse;
> As a world where never rain
> Glittered on the sunny plain;—
> Such, my heart, thy world would be,
> If no love did flow in thee.

> "As a world without the sound
> Of the rivulets underground;
> Or the bubbling of the spring
> Out of darkness wandering;
> Or the mighty rush and flowing
> Of the river's downward going;
> Or the music-showers that drop
> On the outspread beech's top;
> Or the ocean's mighty voice,
> When his lifted waves rejoice;—
> Such, my soul, thy world would be
> If no love did sing in thee.

> "Lady, keep thy world's delight
> Keep the waters in thy sight.
> Love hath made me strong to go,

For thy sake, to realms below,
Where the water's shine and hum
Through the darkness never come:
Let, I pray, one thought of me
Spring, a little well, in thee;
Lest thy loveless soul be found
Like a dry and thirsty ground."

"Sing again, prince. It makes it less tedious," said the princess.

But the prince was too much overcome to sing any more, and a long pause followed.

"This is very kind of you, prince," said the princess at last, quite coolly, as she lay in the boat with her eyes shut.

"I am sorry I can't return the compliment," thought the prince; "but you are worth dying for, after all."

Again a wavelet, and another, and another flowed over the stone, and wetted both the prince's knees; but he did not speak or move. Two—three—four hours passed in this way, the princess apparently asleep, and the prince very patient. But he was much disappointed in his position, for he had none of the consolation he had hoped for.

At last he could bear it no longer.

"Princess!" said he.

But at the moment up started the princess, crying,—
"I'm afloat! I'm afloat!"

And the little boat bumped against the stone.

"Princess!" repeated the prince, encouraged by seeing her wide awake and looking eagerly at the water.

"Well?" said she, without looking round.

"Your papa promised that you should look at me, and you haven't looked at me once."

"Did he? Then I suppose I must. But I am so sleepy!"

"Sleep then, darling, and don't mind me," said the poor prince.

"Really, you are very good," replied the princess. "I think I will go to sleep again."

"Just give me a glass of wine and a biscuit first," said the prince, very humbly.

"With all my heart," said the princess, and gaped as she said it.

She got the wine and the biscuit, however, and leaning over the side of the boat towards him, was compelled to look at him.

"Why, prince," she said, "you don't look well! Are you sure you don't mind it?"

"Not a bit," answered he, feeling very faint indeed. "Only I shall die before it is of any use to you, unless I have something to eat."

"There then," said she, holding out the wine to him.

"Ah! you must feed me. I dare not move my hands. The water would run away directly."

"Good gracious!" said the princess; and she began at once to feed him with bits of biscuit and sips of wine.

As she fed him, he contrived to kiss the tips of her fingers now and then. She did not seem to mind it, one way or the other. But the prince felt better.

"Now, for your own sake, princess," said he, "I cannot let you go to sleep. You must sit and look at me, else I shall not be able to keep up."

"Well, I will do anything to oblige you," answered she, with condescension; and, sitting down, she did look at him, and kept looking at him with wonderful steadiness, considering all things.

The sun went down, and the moon rose, and, gush after gush, the waters were rising up the prince's body. They were up to his waist now.

"Why can't we go and have a swim?" said the princess. "There seems to be water enough just about here."

"I shall never swim more," said the prince.

"Oh, I forgot," said the princess, and was silent.

So the water grew and grew, and rose up and up on the prince. And the princess sat and looked at him. She fed him now and then. The night wore on. The waters rose and rose. The moon rose likewise higher and higher, and shone full on the face of the dying prince. The water was up to his neck.

"Will you kiss me, princess?" said he, feebly. The non-chalance was all gone now.

"Yes, I will," answered the princess, and kissed him with a long, sweet, cold kiss.

"Now," said he, with a sigh of content, "I die happy."

He did not speak again. The princess gave him some wine for the last time: he was past eating. Then she sat down again, and looked at him. The water rose and rose. It touched his chin. It touched his lower lip. It touched between his lips. He shut them hard to keep it out. The princess began to feel strange. It touched his upper lip. He breathed through his nostrils. The princess looked wild. It covered his nostrils. Her eyes looked scared, and shone strange in the moonlight. His head fell back; the water closed over it, and the bubbles of his last breath bubbled up through the water. The princess gave a shriek, and sprang into the lake.

She laid hold first of one leg, and then of the other, and pulled and tugged, but she could not move either. She stopped to take breath, and that made her think that he could not get any breath. She was frantic. She got hold of him, and held his head above the water, which was possible now his hands were no longer on the hole. But it was of no use, for he was past breathing.

Love and water brought back all her strength. She got under the water, and pulled and pulled with her whole might, till at last she got one leg out. The other easily followed. How she got him into the boat she never could tell; but when she did, she fainted away. Coming to herself, she seized the oars, kept herself steady as best she could, and rowed and rowed, though she had never rowed before. Round rocks, and over shallows, and through mud she rowed, till she got to the landing-stairs of the palace. By this time her people were on the shore, for they had heard her shriek. She made them carry the prince to her own room, and lay him in her bed, and light a fire, and send for the doctors.

"But the lake, your highness!" said the chamberlain, who, roused by the noise, came in, in his nightcap.

"Go and drown yourself in it!" she said.

This was the last rudeness of which the princess was ever guilty; and one must allow that she had good cause to feel provoked with the lord chamberlain.

Had it been the king himself, he would have fared no better. But both he and the queen were fast asleep. And the chamberlain went back to his bed. Somehow, the doctors never came. So the princess and her old nurse were left with the prince. But the old nurse was a wise woman, and knew what to do.

They tried everything for a long time without success. The princess was nearly distracted between hope and fear, but she tried on and on, one thing after another, and everything over and over again.

At last, when they had all but given it up, just as the sun rose, the prince opened his eyes.

XV

Look at the Rain!

The princess burst into a passion of tears and *fell* on the floor. There she lay for an hour, and her tears never ceased. All the pent-up crying of her life was spent now. And a rain came on, such as had never been seen in that country. The sun shone all the time, and the great drops, which fell straight to the earth, shone likewise. The palace was in the heart of a rainbow. It was a rain of rubies, and sapphires, and emeralds, and topazes. The torrents poured from the mountains like molten gold; and if it had not been for its subterraneous outlet, the lake would have overflowed and inundated the country. It was full from shore to shore.

But the princess did not heed the lake. She lay on the floor and wept. And this rain within doors was far more wonderful than the rain out of doors. For when it abated a little, and she proceeded to rise, she found, to her astonishment, that she could not. At length, after many efforts, she succeeded in getting upon her feet. But she tumbled down again directly. Hearing her fall, her old nurse uttered a yell of delight, and ran to her, screaming,—

"My darling child! she's found her gravity!"

"Oh, that's it! is it?" said the princess, rubbing her shoulder and her knee alternately. "I consider it very unpleasant. I feel as if I should be crushed to pieces."

"Hurrah!" cried the prince from the bed. "If you've come round, princess, so have I. How's the lake?"

"Brimful," answered the nurse.

"Then we're all happy."

"That we are indeed!" answered the princess, sobbing.

And there was rejoicing all over the country that rainy day. Even the babies forgot their past troubles, and danced and crowed amazingly. And the king told stories, and the queen listened to them. And he divided the money in his box, and she the honey in her pot, among all the children. And there was such jubilation as was never heard of before.

Of course the prince and princess were betrothed at once. But the princess had to learn to walk, before they could be married with any propriety. And this was not so easy at her time of life, for she could walk no more than a baby. She was always falling down and hurting herself.

"Is this the gravity you used to make so much of?" said she one day to the prince, as he raised her from the floor. "For my part, I was a great deal more comfortable without it."

"No, no, that's not it. This is it," replied the prince, as he took her up, and carried her about like a baby, kissing her all the time. "This is gravity."

"That's better," said she. "I don't mind that so much."

And she smiled the sweetest, loveliest smile in the prince's face. And she gave him one little kiss in return for all his; and he thought them overpaid, for he was beside himself with delight. I fear she complained of her gravity more than once after this, notwithstanding.

It was a long time before she got reconciled to walking. But the pain of learning it was quite counterbalanced by two things, either of which would have been sufficient consolation. The first was, that the prince himself was her teacher; and the second, that she could tumble into the lake as often as she pleased. Still, she preferred to have the prince jump in with her; and the splash they made before was nothing to the splash they made now.

The lake never sank again. In process of time, it wore the roof of the cavern quite through, and was twice as deep as before.

The only revenge the princess took upon her aunt was to tread pretty hard on her gouty toe the next time she saw her. But she was sorry for it the very next day, when she heard that the water had undermined her house, and that it had fallen in the night, burying her in its ruins; whence no one ever ventured to dig up her body. There she lies to this day.

So the prince and princess lived and were happy; and

had crowns of gold, and clothes of cloth, and shoes of leather, and children of boys and girls, not one of whom was ever known, on the most critical occasion, to lose the smallest atom of his or her due proportion of gravity.

❧

"The Giant's Heart" also made its first appearance in
MacDonald's Adela Cathcart. *In this story a little girl and
boy wander into Giantland and find themselves threat-
ened by a giant. The giant, however, is lazy and has placed
his heart in the care of the birds of the woods. MacDonald
uses a theme similar to one used in* Phantastes, *which is
that trusting one's heart to someone else leads to a decline
in one's spirit and a loss of humanity.*

CHAPTER TWO

The Giant's Heart

There once was a giant who lived on the borders of Giantland where it touched on the country of common people.

Everything in Giantland was so big that the common people saw only a mass of awful mountains and clouds; and no living man had ever come from it, as far as anybody knew, to tell what he had seen in it.

Somewhere near the borders, on the other side, by the edge of a great forest, lived a labourer with his wife and a great many children. One day Tricksey-Wee, as they called her, teased her brother Buffy-Bob, till he could not bear it any longer, and gave her a box on the ear. Tricksey-Wee cried; and Buffy-Bob was so sorry and so ashamed of himself that he cried too, and ran off into the wood. He was so long gone that Tricksey-Wee began to be frightened, for she was very fond of her brother; and she was so distressed that she had first teased him and then cried, that at last she ran into the wood to look for him, though there was more chance of losing herself than of finding him.

And, indeed, so it seemed likely to turn out; for, running on without looking, she at length found herself in a valley she knew nothing about. And no wonder; for what she thought was a valley with round, rocky sides, was no other than the space between two of the roots of a great tree that grew on the borders of Giantland. She climbed over the side of it, and went towards what she took for a black, round-topped mountain, far away; but which she soon discovered to be close to her, and to be a hollow place so great that she could not tell what it was hollowed out of. Staring at it, she found that it was a doorway; and going nearer and staring harder, she saw the door, far in, with a knocker of iron upon it, a great many yards above her head, and as large as the anchor of a big ship.

Now nobody had ever been unkind to Tricksey-Wee, and therefore she was not afraid of anybody. For Buffy-Bob's box on the ear she did not think worth considering. So spying a little hole at the bottom of the door which had been nibbled by some giant mouse, she crept through it, and found herself in an enormous hall. She could not have seen the other end of it at all, except for the great fire that was burning there, diminished to a spark in the distance. Towards this fire she ran as fast as she could, and was not far from it when something fell before her with a great clatter, over which she tumbled, and went rolling on the floor.

She was not much hurt, however, and got up in a moment. Then she saw that what she had fallen over was not unlike a great iron bucket. When she examined it more closely, she discovered that it was a thimble; and looking up to see who had dropped it, beheld a huge face, with spectacles as big as the round windows in a church, bending over her, and looking everywhere for the thimble. Tricksey-Wee immediately laid hold of it in both her arms, and lifted it about an inch nearer to the nose of the peering giantess. This movement made the old lady see where it was, and, her finger popping into it, it vanished from the eyes of Tricksey-Wee, buried in the folds of a white stocking like a cloud in the sky, which Mrs. Giant was busy darning. For it was Saturday night, and her husband would wear nothing but white stockings on Sunday. To be sure, he did eat little children, but only *very* little ones; and if ever it crossed his mind that it was wrong to do so, he always said to himself that he wore whiter stockings on Sunday than any other giant in all Giantland.

At the same instant Tricksey-Wee heard a sound like the wind in a tree full of leaves, and could not think what it could be; till, looking up, she found that it was the giantess whispering to her; and when she tried very hard she could hear what she said well enough.

"Run away, dear little girl," she said, "as fast as you can; for my husband will be home in a few minutes."

"But I've never been naughty to your husband," said Tricksey-Wee, looking up in the giantess's face.

"That doesn't matter. You had better go. He is fond of little children, particularly little girls."

"Oh, then he won't hurt me."

"I am not sure of that. He is so fond of them that he eats them up; and I am afraid he couldn't help hurting you a little. He's a very good man, though."

"Oh! then—" began Tricksey-Wee, feeling rather frightened; but before she could finish her sentence she heard the sound of footsteps very far apart and very heavy. The next moment, who should come running towards her, full speed, and as pale as death, but Buffy-Bob. She held out her arms, and he ran into them. But when she tried to kiss him, she only kissed the back of his head; for his white face and round eyes were turned to the door.

"Run, children; run and hide," said the giantess.

"Come, Buffy," said Tricksey; "yonder's a great brake; we'll hide in it."

The brake was a big broom; and they had just got into the bristles of it when they heard the door open with a sound of thunder, and in stalked the giant. You would have thought you saw the whole earth through the door when he opened it, so wide was it; and when he closed it, it was like nightfall.

"Where is that little boy?" he cried, with a voice like the bellowing of a cannon. "He looked a very nice boy indeed. I am almost sure he crept through the mouse-hole at the bottom of the door. Where is he, my dear?"

"I don't know," answered the giantess.

"But you know it is wicked to tell lies; don't you, my dear?" retorted the giant.

"Now, you ridiculous old Thunderthump!" said his wife, with a smile as broad as the sea in the sun, "how can I mend your white stockings and look after little boys? You have got plenty to last you over Sunday, I am sure. Just look what good little boys they are!"

Tricksey-Wee and Buffy-Bob peered through the bristles, and discovered a row of little boys, about a dozen, with very fat faces and goggle eyes, sitting before the fire, and looking stupidly into it. Thunderthump intended the most of these for pickling, and was feeding them well before salting them. Now and then, however, he could not keep his teeth off them, and would eat one, by the bye, without salt.

He strode up to the wretched children. Now what made them very wretched indeed was, that they knew if they could only keep from eating, and grow thin, the giant would dislike them, and turn them out to find their way home; but notwithstanding this, so greedy were they, that they ate as much as ever they could hold. The giantess, who fed them, comforted herself with thinking that they were not real boys and girls, but only little pigs pretending to be boys and girls.

"Now tell me the truth," cried the giant, bending his face down over them. They shook with terror, and every one hoped it was somebody else the giant liked best. "Where is the little boy that ran into the hall just now? Whoever tells me a lie shall be instantly boiled."

"He's in the broom," cried one dough-faced boy. "He's in there, and a little girl with him."

"The naughty children," cried the giant, "to hide from *me!*" And he made a stride towards the broom.

"Catch hold of the bristles, Bobby. Get right into a tuft, and hold on," cried Tricksey-Wee, just in time.

The giant caught up the broom, and seeing nothing under it, set it down again with a force that threw them both on the floor. He then made two strides to the boys, caught the dough-faced one by the neck, took the lid off a great pot that was boiling on the fire, popped him in as if he had been a trussed chicken, put the lid on again, and saying, "There, boys! See what comes of lying!" asked no more questions; for, as he always kept his word, he was afraid he might have to do the same to them all; and he did not like boiled boys. He liked to eat them crisp, as radishes, whether forked or not, ought to be eaten. He then sat down, and asked his wife if his supper was ready. She looked into the pot, and throwing the boy out with the ladle, as if he had been a black beetle that had tumbled in and had had the worst of it, answered that she thought it was. Whereupon he rose to help her; and taking the pot from the fire, poured the whole contents, bubbling and splashing, into a dish like a vat. Then they sat down to supper. The children in the broom could not see what they had; but it seemed to agree with them; for the giant talked like thunder, and the giantess answered like the sea, and they grew chattier and chattier. At length the giant said,—

"I don't feel quite comfortable about that heart of mine." And as he spoke, instead of laying his hand on his bosom, he waved it away towards the corner where the children were peeping from the broom bristles, like frightened little mice.

"Well, you know, my darling Thunderthump," answered his wife, "I always thought it ought to be nearer home. But you know best, of course."

"Ha! ha! You don't know where it is, wife. I moved it a month ago."

"What a man you are, Thunderthump! You trust any creature alive rather than your own wife."

Here the giantess gave a sob which sounded exactly like a wave going flop into the mouth of a cave up to the roof.

"Where have you got it now?" she resumed, checking her emotion.

"Well, Doodlem, I don't mind telling *you*," answered the giant, soothingly. "The great she-eagle has got it for a nest egg. She sits on it night and day, and thinks she will bring the greatest eagle out of it that ever sharpened his beak on the rocks of Mount Skycrack. I can warrant no one else will touch it while she has got it. But she is rather capricious, and I confess I am not easy about it; for the least scratch of one of her claws would do for me at once. And she *has* claws."

I refer any one who doubts this part of my story to certain chronicles of Giantland preserved among the Celtic nations. It was quite a common thing for a giant to put his heart out to nurse, because he did not like the trouble and responsibility of doing it himself; although I must confess it was a dangerous sort of plan to take, especially with such a delicate viscus as the heart.

All this time Buffy-Bob and Tricksey-Wee were listening with long ears.

"Oh!" thought Tricksey-Wee, "if I could but find the giant's cruel heart, wouldn't I give it a squeeze!"

The giant and giantess went on talking for a long time. The giantess kept advising the giant to hide his heart somewhere in the house; but he seemed afraid of the advantage it would give her over him.

"You could hide it at the bottom of the flour-barrel," said she.

"That would make me feel chokey," answered he.

"Well, in the coal-cellar. Or in the dust-hole—that's the place! No one would think of looking for your heart in the dust-hole."

"Worse and worse!" cried the giant.

"Well, the water-butt," suggested she.

"No, no; it would grow spongy there," said he.

"Well, what *will* you do with it?"

"I will leave it a month longer where it is, and then I will give it to the Queen of the Kangaroos, and she will carry it in her pouch for me. It is best to change its place, you know, lest my enemies should scent it out. But, dear Doodlem, it's a fretting care to have a heart of one's own to look after. The responsibility is too much for me. If it were not for a bite of a radish now and then, I never could bear it."

Here the giant looked lovingly towards the row of little boys by the fire, all of whom were nodding, or asleep on the floor.

"Why don't you trust it to me, dear Thunderthump?" said his wife. "I would take the best possible care of it."

"I don't doubt it, my love. But the responsibility would be too much for *you*. You would no longer be my darling, light-hearted, airy, laughing Doodlem. It would transform you into a heavy, oppressed woman, weary of life— as I am."

The giant closed his eyes and pretended to go to sleep. His wife got his stockings, and went on with her darning. Soon the giant's pretence became reality, and the giantess began to nod over her work.

"Now, Buffy," whispered Tricksey-Wee, "now's our time. I think it's moonlight, and we had better be off.

There's a door with a hole for the cat just behind us."

"All right," said Bob; "I'm ready."

So they got out of the broom-brake and crept to the door. But to their great disappointment, when they got through it, they found themselves in a sort of shed. It was full of tubs and things, and, though it was built of wood only, they could not find a crack.

"Let us try this hole," said Tricksey; for the giant and giantess were sleeping behind them, and they dared not go back.

"All right," said Bob.

He seldom said anything else than *All right.*

Now this hole was in a mound that came in through the wall of the shed, and went along the floor for some distance. They crawled into it, and found it very dark. But groping their way along, they soon came to a small crack, through which they saw grass, pale in the moonshine. As they crept on, they found the hole began to get wider and lead upwards.

"What is that noise of rushing?" said Buffy-Bob.

"I can't tell," replied Tricksey; "for, you see, I don't know what we are in."

The fact was, they were creeping along a channel in the heart of a giant tree; and the noise they heard was the noise of the sap rushing along in its wooden pipes. When they laid their ears to the wall, they heard it gurgling along with a pleasant noise.

"It sounds kind and good," said Tricksey. "It is water running. Now it must be running from somewhere to somewhere. I think we had better go on, and we shall come somewhere."

It was now rather difficult to go on, for they had to climb as if they were climbing a hill; and now the passage was wide. Nearly worn out, they saw light overhead at last, and creeping through a crack into the open air, found themselves on the fork of a huge tree. A great, broad, uneven space lay around them, out of which spread boughs in every direction, the smallest of them as big as the biggest tree in the country of common people. Overhead were leaves enough to supply all the trees they had ever seen. Not much moonlight could come through, but the leaves would glimmer white in the wind at times. The tree was full of giant birds. Every now and then, one would sweep through, with a great noise. But, except an occasional chirp, sounding like a shrill pipe in a great organ, they made no noise. All at once an owl began to hoot. He thought he was singing. As soon as he began, other birds replied, making rare game of him. To their astonishment, the children found they could understand every word they sang. And what they sang was something like this:

> "I will sing a song.
>   I'm the owl."
> "Sing a song, you sing-song
>   Ugly fowl!
>   What will you sing about,
>   Night in and Day out?"
>
> "Sing about the night;
>   I'm the owl."
> "You could not see for the light,
>   Stupid fowl!"
> "Oh! the moon! and the dew!
>   And the shadows!—tu-whoo!"

The owl spread out his silent, soft, sly wings, and lighting between Tricksey-Wee and Buffy-Bob, nearly smothered them, closing up one under each wing. It was like being buried in a down bed. But the owl did not like anything between his sides and his wings, so he opened his wings again, and the children made haste to get out.

Tricksey-Wee immediately went in front of the bird, and looking up into his huge face, which was as round as the eyes of the giantess's spectacles, and much bigger, dropped a pretty courtesy, and said,—

"Please, Mr. Owl, I want to whisper to you."

"Very well, small child," answered the owl, looking important, and stooping his ear towards her. "What is it?"

"Please tell me where the eagle lives that sits on the giant's heart."

"Oh, you naughty child! That's a secret. For shame!"

And with a great hiss that terrified them, the owl flew into the tree. All birds are fond of secrets; but not many of them can keep them so well as the owl.

So the children went on because they did not know what else to do. They found the way very rough and difficult, the tree was so full of humps and hollows. Now and then they plashed into a pool of rain; now and then they came upon twigs growing out of the trunk where they had no business, and they were as large as full-grown poplars. Sometimes they came upon great cushions of soft moss, and on one of them they lay down and rested. But they had not lain long before they spied a large nightingale sitting on a branch, with its bright eyes looking up at the moon. In a moment more he began to sing, and the birds about him began to reply, but in a very different tone from that in which they had replied to the owl. Oh, the birds did call the nightingale such pretty names! The nightingale sang, and the birds replied like this:—

> "I will sing a song.
>   I'm the nightingale."
> "Sing a song, long, long,
>   Little Neverfail!
> What will you sing about,
> Light in or light out?"

"Sing about the light
    Gone away;
Down, away, and out of sight—
    Poor lost day!
Mourning for the day dead,
O'er his dim bed."

The nightingale sang so sweetly, that the children would have fallen asleep but for fear of losing any of the song. When the nightingale stopped they got up and wandered on. They did not know where they were going, but they thought it best to keep going on, because then they might come upon something or other. They were very sorry they had forgotten to ask the nightingale about the eagle's nest, but his music had put everything else out of their heads. They resolved, however, not to forget the next time they had a chance. So they went on and on, till they were both tired, and Tricksey-Wee said at last, trying to laugh,—

"I declare my legs feel like a Dutch doll's."

"Then here's the place to go to bed in," said Buffy-Bob.

They stood at the edge of a last year's nest, and looked down with delight into the round, mossy cave. Then they crept gently in, and, lying down in each other's arms, found it so deep, and warm, and comfortable, and soft, that they were soon fast asleep.

Now close beside them, in a hollow, was another nest, in which lay a lark and his wife; and the children were awakened, very early in the morning, by a dispute between Mr. and Mrs. Lark.

"Let me up," said the lark.

"It is not time," said the lark's wife.

"It is," said the lark, rather rudely. "The darkness is quite thin. I can almost see my own beak."

"Nonsense!" said the lark's wife. "You know you

came home yesterday morning quite worn out—you had to fly so very high before you saw him. I am sure he would not mind if you took it a little easier. Do be quiet and go to sleep again."

"That's not it at all," said the lark. "He doesn't want me. I want him. Let me up, I say."

He began to sing; and Tricksey-Wee and Buffy-Bob, having now learned the way, answered him:—

> "I will sing a song
>   I'm the Lark."
> "Sing, sing, Throat-song,
>   Little Kill-the-dark.
> What will you sing about,
>   Now the night is out?"

> "I can only call;
>   I can't think.
> Let me up—that's all.
>   Let me drink!
> Thirsting all the long night
> For a drink of light."

By this time the lark was standing on the edge of his nest and looking at the children.

"Poor little things! You can't fly," said the lark.

"No; but we can look up," said Tricksey.

"Ah, you don't know what it is to see the very first of the sun."

"But we know what it is to wait till he comes. He's no worse for your seeing him first, is he?"

"Oh no, certainly not," answered the lark, with condescension; and then, bursting into his *Jubilate*, he sprang aloft, clapping his wings like a clock running down.

"Tell us where—" began Buffy-Bob.

But the lark was out of sight. His song was all that was left of him. That was everywhere, and he was nowhere.

"Selfish bird!" said Buffy. "It's all very well for larks to go hunting the sun, but they have no business to despise their neighbours, for all that."

"Can I be of any service to you?" said a sweet bird-voice out of the nest.

This was the lark's wife, who stayed at home with the young larks while her husband went to church.

"Oh! thank you. If you please," answered Tricksey-Wee.

And up popped a pretty brown head; and then up came a brown feathery body; and last of all came the slender legs on to the edge of the nest. There she turned, and, looking down into the nest, from which came a whole litany of chirpings for breakfast, said, "Lie still, little ones." Then she turned to the children.

"My husband is King of the Larks," she said.

Buffy-Bob took off his cap, and Tricksey-Wee courtesied very low.

"Oh, it's not me," said the bird, looking very shy. "I am only his wife. It's my husband."

And she looked up after him into the sky, whence his song was still falling like a shower of musical hailstones. Perhaps *she* could see him.

"He's a splendid bird," said Buffy-Bob; "only you know he *will* get up a little too early."

"Oh, no! he doesn't. It's only his way, you know. But tell me what I can do for you."

"Tell us, please, Lady Lark, where the she-eagle lives that sits on Giant Thunderthump's heart."

"Oh! that is a secret."

"Did you promise not to tell?"

"No; but larks ought to be discreet. They see more than other birds."

"But you don't fly up high like your husband, do you?"

"Not often. But it's no matter. I come to know things for all that."

"Do tell me, and I will sing you a song," said Tricksey-Wee.

"Can you sing too?—You have got no wings!"

"Yes. And I will sing you a song I learned the other day about a lark and his wife."

"Please do," said the lark's wife. "Be quiet, children, and listen."

Tricksey-Wee was very glad she happened to know a song which would please the lark's wife, at least, whatever the lark himself might have thought of it if he had heard it. So she sang:—

"Good-morrow, my lord!" in the sky alone,
Sang the lark, as the sun ascended his throne.
"Shine on me, my lord; I only am come,
Of all your servants, to welcome you home.
I have flown a whole hour, right up, I swear,
To catch the first shine of your golden hair!"

"Must I thank you, then," said the king, "Sir Lark,
For flying so high, and hating the dark?
You ask a full cup for half a thirst:
Half is love of me, and half love to be first.
There's many a bird that makes no haste,
But waits till I come. That's as much to my taste."

And the king hid his head in a turban of cloud;
And the lark stopped singing, quite vexed and cowed
But he flew up higher and thought, "Anon,
The wrath of the king will be over and gone;
And his crown, shining out of its cloudy fold,
Will change my brown feathers to a glory of gold."

So he flew, with the strength of a lark he flew,
But as he rose the cloud rose too;
And not a gleam of the golden hair
Came through the depth of the misty air;
Till, weary with flying, with sighing sore,
The strong sun-seeker could do no more.

His wings had no chrism of gold,
And his feathers felt withered and worn and old;
So he quivered and sank, and dropped like a stone
And there on his nest, where he left her, alone,
Sat his little wife on her little eggs,
Keeping them warm with wings and legs.

Did I say alone? Ah, no such thing!
Full in her face was shining the king.
"Welcome, Sir Lark! You look tired," said he:
"*Up* is not always the best way to me.
While you have been singing so high and away,
I've been shining to your little wife all day."

He had set his crown all about the nest,
And out of the midst shone her little brown breast;
And so glorious was she in russet gold,
That for wonder and awe Sir Lark grew cold.
He popped his head under her wing, and lay
As still as a stone, till the king was away.

As soon as Tricksey-Wee had finished her song, the
lark's wife began a low, sweet, modest little song of her
own; and after she had piped away for two or three
minutes, she said,—

"You dear children, what can I do for you?"

"Tell us where the she-eagle lives, please," said
Tricksey-Wee.

"Well, I don't think there can be much harm in telling
such wise, good children," said Lady Lark; "I am sure
you don't want to do any mischief."

"Oh, no; quite the contrary," said Buffy-Bob.

"Then I'll tell you. She lives on the very topmost peak
of Mount Skycrack; and the only way to get up is to
climb on the spider's webs that cover it from top to bottom."

"That's rather serious," said Tricksey-Wee.

"But you don't want to go up, you foolish little thing! You can't go. And what do you want to go up for?"

"That is a secret," said Tricksey-Wee.

"Well, it's no business of mine," rejoined Lady Lark, a little offended, and quite vexed that she had told them. So she flew away to find some breakfast for her little ones, who by this time were chirping very impatiently. The children looked at each other, joined hands, and walked off.

In a minute more the sun was up, and they soon reached the outside of the tree. The bark was so knobby and rough, and full of twigs, that they managed to get down, though not without great difficulty. Then, far away to the north they saw a huge peak, like the spire of a church, going right up into the sky. They thought this must be Mount Skycrack, and turned their faces towards it. As they went on, they saw a giant or two, now and then, striding about the fields or through the woods, but they kept out of their way. Nor were they in much danger; for it was only one or two of the border giants that were so very fond of children.

At last they came to the foot of Mount Skycrack. It stood in a plain alone, and shot right up, I don't know how many thousand feet, into the air, a long, narrow, spearlike mountain. The whole face of it, from top to bottom, was covered with a network of spiders' webs, the threads of various sizes, from that of silk to that of whipcord. The webs shook, and quivered, and waved in the sun, glittering like silver. All about ran huge greedy spiders, catching huge silly flies, and devouring them.

Here they sat down to consider what could be done. The spiders did not heed them, but ate away at the flies.—Now at the foot of the mountain, and all around it, was a ring of water, not very broad, but very deep. As they sat watching them, one of the spiders, whose web was woven across this water, somehow or other lost his

hold, and fell in on his back. Tricksey-Wee and Buffy-Bob
ran to his assistance, and laying hold each of one of his
legs, succeeded, with the help of the other legs, which
struggled spiderfully, in getting him out upon dry land.
As soon as he had shaken himself, and dried himself a
little, the spider turned to the children, saying,—

"And now, what can I do for you?"

"Tell us, please," said they, "how we can get up the
mountain to the she-eagle's nest."

"Nothing is easier," answered the spider. "Just run up
there, and tell them all I sent you, and nobody will mind
you."

"But we haven't got claws like you, Mr. Spider," said
Buffy.

"Ah! no more you have, poor unprovided creatures!
Still, I think we can manage it. Come home with me."

"You won't eat us, will you?" said Buffy.

"My dear child," answered the spider, in a tone of in-
jured dignity, "I eat nothing but what is mischievous or
useless. You have helped me, and now I will help you."

The children rose at once, and climbing as well as they
could, reached the spider's nest in the centre of the web.
Nor did they find it very difficult; for whenever too great
a gap came, the spider spinning a strong cord stretched
it just where they would have chosen to put their feet
next. He left them in his nest, after bringing them two
enormous honey-bags, taken from bees that he had
caught; but presently about six of the wisest of the spiders came back with him. It was rather horrible to look
up and see them all around the mouth of the nest, looking down on them in contemplation, as if wondering
whether they would be nice eating. At length one of them
said,—"Tell us truly what you want with the eagle, and
we will try to help you."

Then Tricksey-Wee told them that there was a giant on
the borders who treated little children no better than

radishes, and that they had narrowly escaped being
eaten by him; that they had found out that the great she-
eagle of Mount Skycrack was at present sitting on his
heart; and that, if they could only get hold of the heart,
they would soon teach the giant better behaviour."

"But," said their host, "if you get at the heart of the
giant, you will find it as large as one of your elephants.
What can you do with it?"

"The least scratch will kill," replied Buffy-Bob.

"Ah! but you might do better than that," said the
spider.—"Now we have resolved to help you. Here is a
little bag of spider-juice. The giants cannot bear spiders,
and this juice is dreadful poison to them. We are all
ready to go up with you, and drive the eagle away. Then
you must put the heart into this other bag, and bring it
down with you; for then the giant will be in your power."

"But how can we do that?" said Buffy. "The bag is not
much bigger than a pudding-bag."

"But it is as large as you will be able to carry."

"Yes; but what are we to do with the heart?"

"Put it into the bag, to be sure. Only, first, you must
squeeze a drop out of the other bag upon it. You will see
what will happen."

"Very well; we will do as you tell us," said Tricksey-
Wee. "And now, if you please, how shall we go?"

"Oh, that's our business," said the first spider. "You
come with me, and my grandfather will take your
brother. Get up."

So Tricksey-Wee mounted on the narrow part of the
spider's back, and held fast. And Buffy-Bob got on the
grandfather's back. And up they scrambled, over one
web after another, up and up—so fast! And every spider
followed; so that when Tricksey-Wee looked back, she
saw a whole army of spiders scrambling after them.

"What can we want with so many?" she thought; but
she said nothing.

The moon was now up, and it was a splendid sight below and around them. All Giantland was spread out under them, with its great hills, lakes, trees, and animals. And all above them was the clear heaven, and Mount Skycrack rising into it, with its endless ladders of spiderwebs, glittering like cords made of moonbeams. And up the moonbeams went, crawling and scrambling, and racing, a huge army of huge spiders.

At length they reached all but the very summit, where they stopped. Tricksey-Wee and Buffy-Bob could see above them a great globe of feathers, that finished off the mountain like an ornamental knob.

"But how shall we drive her off?" said Buffy.

"We'll soon manage that," answered the grandfather-spider. "Come on, you down there."

Up rushed the whole army, past the children, over the edge of the nest, on to the she-eagle, and buried themselves in her feathers. In a moment she became very restless, and went pecking about with her beak. All at once she spread out her wings, with a sound like a whirlwind, and flew off to bathe in the sea; and then the spiders began to drop from her in all directions on their gossamer wings. The children had to hold fast to keep the wind of the eagle's flight from blowing them off. As soon as it was over, they looked into the nest, and there lay the giant's heart—an awful and ugly thing.

"Make haste, child!" said Tricksey's spider.

So Tricksey took her bag, and squeezed a drop out of it upon the heart. She thought she heard the giant give a far-off roar of pain, and she nearly fell from her seat with terror. The heart instantly began to shrink. It shrunk and shrivelled till it was nearly gone; and Buffy-Bob caught it up and put it into his bag. Then the two spiders turned and went down again as fast as they could. Before they got to the bottom, they heard the shrieks of the she-eagle over the loss of her egg; but the spiders told them not to be alarmed, for her eyes were too big to see them.—By the time they reached the foot of the mountain, all the spiders had got home, and were busy again catching flies, as if nothing had happened.

After renewed thanks to their friends, the children set off, carrying the giant's heart with them.

"If you should find it at all troublesome, just give it a little more spider-juice directly," said the grandfather, as they took their leave.

Now the giant had given an awful roar of pain the moment they anointed his heart, and had fallen down in a fit, in which he lay so long that all the boys might have escaped if they had not been so fat. One did, and got home in safety. For days the giant was unable to speak. The first words he uttered were,—

"Oh, my heart! my heart!"

"Your heart is safe enough, dear Thunderthump," said his wife. "Really, a man of your size ought not to be so nervous and apprehensive. I am ashamed of you."

"You have no heart, Doodlem," answered he. "I assure you at this moment mine is in the greatest danger. It has fallen into the hands of foes, though who they are I cannot tell."

Here he fainted again; for Tricksey-Wee, finding the heart beginning to swell a little, had given the least touch of spider-juice.

Again he recovered, and said,—

"Dear Doodlem, my heart is coming back to me. It is coming nearer and nearer."

After lying silent for hours, he exclaimed,—

"It is in the house, I know!"

And he jumped up and walked about, looking in every corner.

As he arose, Tricksey-Wee and Buffy-Bob came out of the hole in the tree-root, and through the cat-hole in the door, and walked boldly towards the giant. Both kept their eyes busy watching him. Led by the love of his own heart, the giant soon spied them, and staggered furiously towards them.

"I will eat you, you vermin!" he cried. "Here with my heart!"

Tricksey gave the heart a sharp pinch. Down fell the giant on his knees, blubbering, and crying, and begging for his heart.

"You shall have it, if you behave yourself properly," said Tricksey.

"How shall I behave myself properly?" asked he, whimpering.

"Take all those boys and girls, and carry them home at once."

"I'm not able; I'm too ill. I shall fall down."

"Take them up directly."

"I can't, till you give me my heart."

"Very well!" said Tricksey; and she gave the heart another pinch.

The giant jumped to his feet, and catching up all the children, thrust some into his waistcoat-pockets, some into his breast-pocket, put two or three into his hat, and took a bundle of them under each arm. Then he staggered to the door.

All this time poor Doodlem was sitting in her armchair, crying, and mending a white stocking.

The giant led the way to the borders. He could not go so fast but that Buffy and Tricksey managed to keep up with him. When they reached the borders, they thought it would be safer to let the children find their own way home. So they told him to set them down. He obeyed.

"Have you put them all down, Mr. Thunderthump?" asked Tricksey-Wee.

"Yes," said the giant.

"That's a lie!" squeaked a little voice; and out came a head from his waistcoat pocket.

Tricksey-Wee pinched the heart till the giant roared with pain.

"You're not a gentleman. You tell stories," she said.

"He was the thinnest of the lot," said Thunderthump, crying.

"Are you all there now, children?" asked Tricksey.

"Yes, ma'am," returned they, after counting themselves very carefully, and with some difficulty; for they were all stupid children.

"Now," said Tricksey-Wee to the giant, "will you promise to carry off no more children, and never to eat a child again all your life?"

"Yes, yes! I promise," answered Thunderthump, sobbing.

"And you will never cross the borders of Giantland?"

"Never."

"And you will never again wear white stockings on a Sunday, all your life long.—Do you promise?"

The giant hesitated at this, and began to expostulate; but Tricksey-Wee, believing it would be good for his morals, insisted; and the giant promised.

Then she required of him, that, when she gave him back his heart, he should give it to his wife to take care of for him forever after. The poor giant fell on his knees, and began again to beg. But Tricksey-Wee giving the heart a slight pinch, he bawled out,—

"Yes, yes! Doodlem shall have it, I swear. Only she must not put it in the flour-barrel, or in the dust-hole."

"Certainly not. Make your own bargain with her.—And you promise not to interfere with my brother and me, or to take any revenge for what we have done?"

"Yes, yes, my dear children; I promise everything. Do, pray, make haste and give me back my poor heart."

"Wait there, then, till I bring it to you."

"Yes, yes. Only make haste, for I feel very faint."

Tricksey-Wee began to undo the mouth of the bag. But

Buffy-Bob, who had got very knowing on his travels, took out his knife with the pretence of cutting the string; but, in reality, to be prepared for any emergency.

No sooner was the heart out of the bag, than it expanded to the size of a bullock; and the giant, with a yell of rage and vengeance, rushed on the two children, who had stepped sideways from the terrible heart. But Buffy-Bob was too quick for Thunderthump. He sprang to the heart, and buried his knife in it, up to the hilt. A fountain of blood spouted from it; and with a dreadful groan the giant fell dead at the feet of little Tricksey-Wee, who could not help being sorry for him, after all.

❧

"The Shadows" is another story that originally appeared in Adela Cathcart. *This time the story is about a sick old man who, being between life and death, has a vision of fairies carrying him away to the Land of Shadows. While there he is taught about how shadows often help men grow spiritually. Shadows frighten men when they are doing wrong, and so shadows, being part of God's creation, have a positive moral effect upon men.*

CHAPTER THREE
_____

The Shadows

Old Ralph Rinkelmann made his living by comic sketches, and all but lost it again by tragic poems. So he was just the man to be chosen king of the fairies, for in Fairyland the sovereignty is elective.

It is no doubt very strange that fairies should desire to have a mortal king; but the fact is, that with all their knowledge and power, they cannot get rid of the feeling that some men are greater than they are, though they can neither fly nor play tricks. So at such times as there happens to be twice the usual number of sensible electors, such a man as Ralph Rinkelmann gets to be chosen.

They did not mean to insist on his residence; for they needed his presence only on special occasions. But they must get hold of him somehow, first of all, in order to make him king. Once he was crowned, they could get him as often as they pleased; but before this ceremony, there was a difficulty. For it is only between life and death that the fairies have power over grown-up mortals, and can carry them off to their country. So they had to watch for an opportunity.

Nor had they to wait long. For old Ralph was taken dreadfully ill; and while hovering between life and death, they carried him off, and crowned him King of Fairyland. But after he was crowned, it was no wonder, considering the state of his health, that he should not be able to sit quite upright on the throne of Fairyland; or that, in consequence, all the gnomes and goblins, and ugly, cruel things that live in the holes and corners of the kingdom, should take advantage of his condition, and run quite wild, playing him, king as he was, all sorts of tricks; crowding about his throne, climbing up the steps, and actually scrambling and quarrelling like mice about his ears and eyes, so that he could see and think of nothing else. But I am not going to tell anything more about this part of his adventures just at present. By strong and sustained efforts he succeeded, after much trouble and suffering, in reducing his rebellious subjects to order. They all vanished to their respective holes and corners; and King Ralph, coming to himself, found himself in his bed, half propped up with pillows.

But the room was full of dark creatures, which gambolled about in the firelight in such a strange, huge, though noiseless fashion, that he thought at first that some of his rebellious goblins had not been subdued with the rest, but had followed him beyond the bounds of Fairyland into his own private house in London. How else could these mad, grotesque hippopotamus-calves make their ugly appearance in Ralph Rinkelmann's bedroom?

But he soon found out that although they were like the underground goblins, they were very different as well, and would require quite different treatment. He felt convinced that they were his subjects too, but that he must have overlooked them somehow at his late coronation—if indeed they had been present; for he could not recollect that he had seen anything just like them before.

He resolved, therefore, to pay particular attention to their habits, ways, and characters; else he saw plainly that they would soon be too much for him; as indeed this intrusion into his chamber, where Mrs. Rinkelmann, who must be queen if he was king, sat taking some tea by the fireside, evidently foreshadowed. But she, perceiving that he was looking about him with a more composed expression than his face had worn for many days, started up, and came quickly and quietly to his side, and her face was bright with gladness. Whereupon the fire burned up more cheerily; and the figures became more composed and respectful in their behaviour, retreating towards the wall like well-trained attendants. Then the king of Fairyland had some tea and dry toast, and leaning back on his pillows, nearly fell asleep; but not quite, for he still watched the intruders.

Presently the queen left the room to give some of the young princes and princesses their tea; and the fire burned lower, and behold, the figures grew as black and as mad in their gambols as ever! Their favourite games seemed to be *Hide and Seek; Touch and Go; Grin and Vanish:* and many other such; and all in the king's bedchamber, too; so that it was quite alarming. It was almost as bad as if the house had been haunted by certain creatures which shall be nameless in a fairy story, because with them Fairyland will not willingly have much to do.

"But it is a mercy that they have their slippers on!" said the king to himself; for his head ached.

As he lay back, with his eyes half shut and half open, too tired to pay longer attention to their games, but, on the whole, considerably more amused than offended with the liberties they took, for they seemed good-natured creatures, and more frolicsome and positively ill-mannered, he became suddenly aware that two of them had stepped forward from the walls, upon which,

after the manner of great spiders, most of them preferred sprawling, and now stood in the middle of the
floor at the foot of his majesty's bed, becking and bow-
ing and ducking in the most grotesquely obsequious
manner; while every now and then they turned solemnly
round upon one heel, evidently considering that motion
the highest token of homage they could show.

"What do you want?" said the king.

"That it may please your majesty to be better acquainted with us," answered they. "We are your majesty's subjects."

"I know you are. I shall be most happy," answered the
king.

"We are not what your majesty takes us for, though.
We are not so foolish as your majesty thinks us."

"It is impossible to take you for anything that I know
of," rejoined the king, who wished to make them talk,
and said whatever came uppermost;—"for soldiers, sail-
ors, or anything: you will not stand still long enough. I
suppose you really belong to the fire brigade; at least,
you keep putting its light out."

"Don't jest, please your majesty." And as they said the
words—for they both spoke at once throughout the
interview—they performed a grave somerset towards
the king.

"Not jest!" retorted he; "and with you? Why, you do
nothing but jest. What are you?"

"The Shadows, sire. And when we do jest, sire, we
always jest in earnest. But perhaps your majesty does
not see us distinctly."

"I see you perfectly well," returned the king.

"Permit me, however," rejoined one of the Shadows;
and as he spoke he approached the king; and lifting a
dark forefinger, he drew it lightly but carefully across
the ridge of his forehead, from temple to temple. The
king felt the soft gliding touch go, like water, into every
hollow, and over the top of every height of that

mountain-chain of thought. He had involuntarily closed his eyes during the operation, and when he unclosed them again, as soon as the finger was withdrawn, he found that they were opened in more senses than one. The room appeared to have extended itself on all sides, till he could not exactly see where the walls were; and all about it stood the Shadows, motionless. They were tall and solemn; rather awful, indeed, in their appearance, notwithstanding many remarkable traits of grotesqueness, for they looked just like the pictures of Puritans drawn by Cavaliers, with long arms, and very long, thin legs, from which hung large loose feet, while in their countenances length of chin and nose predominated. The solemnity of their mien, however, overcame all the oddity of their form, so that they were very *eerie* indeed to look at, dressed as they all were in funeral black.

But a single glance was all that the king was allowed to have; for the former operator waved his dusky palm across his vision, and once more the king saw only the fire-lighted walls, and dark shapes flickering about upon them. The two who had spoken for the rest seemed likewise to have vanished. But at last the king discovered them, standing one on each side of the fireplace. They kept close to the chimney-wall, and talked to each other across the length of the chimney-piece; thus avoiding the direct rays of the fire, which, though light is necessary to their appearing to human eyes, do not agree with them at all—much less give birth to them, as the king was soon to learn. After a few minutes they again approached the bed, and spoke thus:

"It is now getting dark, please your majesty. We mean, out of doors in the snow. Your majesty may see, from where he is lying, the cold light of its great winding-sheet—a famous carpet for the Shadows to dance upon, your majesty. All our brothers and sisters will be at church now, before going to their night's work."

"Do they always go to church before they go to work?"

"They always go to church first."

"Where is the church?"

"In Iceland. Would your majesty like to see it?"

"How can I go and see it, when, as you know very well, I am ill in bed? Besides, I should be sure to take cold in a frosty night like this, even if I put on the blankets, and took the feather-bed for a muff."

A sort of quivering passed over their faces, which seemed to be their mode of laughing. The whole shape of the face shook and fluctuated as if it had been some dark fluid; till, by slow degrees of gathering calm, it settled into its former rest. Then one of them drew aside the curtains of the bed, and the window-curtains not having been yet drawn, the king beheld the white glimmering night outside, struggling with the heaps of darkness that tried to quench it; and the heavens full of stars, flashing and sparkling like live jewels. The other Shadows went towards the fire and vanished in it.

Scores of Shadows immediately began an insane dance all about the room; disappearing, one after the other, through the uncovered window, and gliding darkly away over the face of the white snow; for the window looked at once on a field of snow. In a few moments the room was quite cleared of them; but instead of being relieved by their absence, the king felt immediately as if he were in a dead-house, and could hardly breathe for the sense of emptiness and desolation that fell upon him. But as he lay looking out on the snow, which stretched blank and wide before him, he spied in the distance a long dark line which drew nearer and nearer, and showed itself at last to be all the Shadows, walking in a double row, and carrying in the midst of them something like a bier. They vanished under the window, but soon reappeared, having somehow climbed up the wall of the house; for they entered in perfect order by the window, as if melting through the transparency of the glass.

They still carried the bier or litter. It was covered with richest furs, and skins of gorgeous wild beasts, whose eyes were replaced by sapphires and emeralds, that glittered and gleamed in the fire and snow light. The outermost skin sparkled with frost, but the inside ones were soft and warm and dry as the down under a swan's wing. The Shadows approached the bed, and set the litter upon it. Then a number of them brought a huge fur robe, and wrapping it round the king, laid him on the litter in the midst of the furs. Nothing could be more gentle and respectful than the way in which they moved him; and he never thought of refusing to go. Then they put something on his head, and, lifting the litter, carried him once round the room, to fall into order.

As he passed the mirror he saw that he was covered with royal ermine, and that his head wore a wonderful crown of gold, set with none but red stones: rubies and carbuncles and garnets, and others whose names he could not tell, glowed gloriously around his head, like the salamandrine essence of all the Christmas fires over the world. A sceptre lay beside him—a rod of ebony, surmounted by a cone-shaped diamond, which, cut in a hundred facets, flashed all the hues of the rainbow, and threw coloured gleams on every side, that looked like Shadows too, but more ethereal than those that bore him.

Then the Shadows rose gently to the window, passed through it, and sinking slowly upon the field of outstretched snow, commenced an orderly gliding rather than march along the frozen surface. They took it by turns to bear the king, as they sped with the swiftness of thought, in a straight line towards the north. The pole-star rose above their heads with visible rapidity; for indeed they moved quite as fast as sad thoughts, though not with all the speed of happy desires. England and Scotland slid past the litter of the king of the Shadows.

Over rivers and lakes they skimmed and glided. They climbed the high mountains, and crossed the valleys with a fearless bound; till they came to John-o'-Groat's house and the Northern Sea. The sea was not frozen; for all the stars shone as clear out of the deeps below as they shone out of the deeps above; and as the bearers slid along the blue-gray surface, with never a furrow in their track, so pure was the water beneath, that the king saw neither surface, bottom, nor substance to it, and seemed to be gliding only through the blue sphere of heaven, with the stars above him, and the stars below him, and between the stars and him nothing but an emptiness, where, for the first time in his life, his soul felt that it had room enough.

At length they reached the rocky shores of Iceland. There they landed, still pursuing their journey. All this time the king felt no cold; for the red stones in his crown kept him warm, and the emerald and sapphire eyes of the wild beasts kept the frosts from settling upon his litter.

Oftentimes upon their way they had to pass through forests, caverns, and rock-shadowed paths, where it was so dark that at first the king feared he should lose his Shadows altogether. But as soon as they entered such places, the diamond in his sceptre began to shine, and glow, and flash, sending out streams of light of all the colours that the painter's soul could dream of; in which light the Shadows grew livelier and stronger than ever, speeding through the dark ways with an all but blinding swiftness. In the light of the diamond, too, some of their forms became more simple and human, while others seemed only to break out into a yet more untamable absurdity.

Once, as they passed through a cave, the king actually saw some of their eyes—strange shadow-eyes: he had never seen any of their eyes before. But at the same moment when he saw their eyes, he knew their faces too, for they turned them full upon him for an instant; and the other Shadows, catching sight of these, shrank and shivered, and nearly vanished. Lovely faces they were; but the king was very thoughtful after he saw them, and continued rather troubled all the rest of the journey. He could not account for those faces being there, and the faces of Shadows, too, with living eyes.

But he soon found that amongst the Shadows a man must learn never to be surprised at anything; for if he does not, he will soon grow quite stupid, in consequence of the endless recurrence of surprises.

At last they climbed up the bed of a little stream, and then, passing through a narrow rocky defile, came out suddenly upon the side of a mountain, overlooking a blue frozen lake in the very heart of mighty hills. Overhead, the *aurora borealis* was shivering and flashing like a battle of ten thousand spears. Underneath, its beams passed faintly over the blue ice and the sides of the snow-clad mountains, whose tops shot up like huge icicles all about, with here and there a star sparkling on the very tip of one. But as the northern lights in the sky above, so wavered and quivered, and shot hither and thither, the Shadows on the surface of the lake below; now gathering in groups, and now shivering asunder; now covering the whole surface of the lake, and anon condensed into one dark knot in the centre. Every here and there on the white mountains might be seen two or three shooting away towards the tops, to vanish beyond them, so that their number was gradually, though not visibly, diminishing.

"Please your majesty," said the Shadows, "this is our church—the Church of the Shadows."

And so saying, the king's body-guard set down the litter upon a rock, and plunged into the multitudes below. They soon returned, however, and bore the king down into the middle of the lake. All the Shadows came crowding round him, respectfully but fearlessly; and sure never such a grotesque assembly revealed itself before to mortal eyes. The king had seen all kinds of gnomes, goblins, and kobolds at his coronation; but they were quite rectilinear figures compared with the insane lawlessness of form in which the Shadows rejoiced; and the wildest gambols of the former were orderly dances of ceremony beside the apparently aimless and wilful contortions of figure, and metamorphoses of shape, in which the latter indulged. They retained, however, all the time, to the surprise of the king, an identity, each of his own type, inexplicably perceptible through every change. Indeed, this preservation of the primary idea of each form was more wonderful than the bewildering and ridiculous alterations to which the form itself was every moment subjected.

"What are you?" said the king, leaning on his elbow, and looking around him.

"The Shadows, your majesty," answered several voices at once.

"What Shadows?"

"The human Shadows. The Shadows of men, and women, and their children."

"Are you not the shadows of chairs and tables, and pokers and tongs, just as well?"

At this question a strange jarring commotion went through the assembly with a shock. Several of the figures shot up as high as the aurora, but instantly settled down again to human size, as if overmastering their feelings, out of respect to him who had roused them. One who had bounded to the highest visible icy peak, and as suddenly returned, now elbowed his way through the rest, and made himself spokesman for them during the remaining part of the dialogue.

"Excuse our agitation, your majesty," said he. "I see

your majesty has not yet thought proper to make himself acquainted with our nature and habits."

"I wish to do so now," replied the king.

"We are the Shadows," repeated the Shadow, solemnly.

"Well?" said the king.

"We do not often appear to men."

"Ha!" said the king.

"We do not belong to the sunshine at all. We go through it unseen, and only by a passing chill do men recognise an unknown presence."

"Ha!" said the king again.

"It is only in the twilight of the fire, or when one man or woman is alone with a single candle, or when any number of people are all feeling the same thing at once, making them one, that we show ourselves, and the truth of things."

"Can that be true that loves the night?" said the king.

"The darkness is the nurse of light," answered the Shadow.

"Can that be true which mocks at forms?" said the king.

"Truth rides abroad in shapeless storms," answered the Shadow.

"Ha! ha!" thought Ralph Rinkelmann, "it rhymes. The Shadow caps my questions with his answers. Very strange!" And he grew thoughtful again.

The Shadow was the first to resume.

"Please your majesty, may we present our petition?"

"By all means," replied the king. "I am not well enough to receive it in proper state."

"Never mind, your majesty. We do not care for much ceremony; and indeed none of us are quite well at present. The subject of our petition weighs upon us."

"Go on," said the king.

"Sire," began the Shadow, "our very existence is in

danger. The various sorts of artificial light, both in houses and in men, women, and children, threaten to end our being. The use and the disposition of gaslights, especially high in the centres, blind the eyes by which alone we can be perceived. We are all but banished from towns. We are driven into villages and lonely houses, chiefly old farm-houses, out of which even our friends the fairies are fast disappearing. We therefore petition our king, by the power of his art to restore us to our rights in the house itself, and in the hearts of its inhabitants."

"But," said the king, "you frighten the children."

"Very seldom, your majesty; and then only for their good. We seldom seek to frighten anybody. We mostly want to make people silent and thoughtful; to awe them a little, your majesty."

"You are much more likely to make them laugh," said the king.

"Are we?" said the Shadow.

And approaching the king one step, he stood quite still for a moment. The diamond of the king's sceptre shot out a vivid flame of violet light, and the king stared at the Shadow in silence, and his lip quivered. He never told what he saw then; but he would say:

"Just fancy what it might be if *some* flitting thoughts were to persist in staying to be looked at."

"It is only," resumed the Shadow, "when our thoughts are not fixed upon any particular object, that our bodies are subject to all the vagaries of elemental influences. Generally, amongst worldly men and frivolous women, we only attach ourselves to some article of furniture or of dress; and they never doubt that we are mere foolish and vague results of the dashing of the waves of the light against the solid forms of which their houses are full. We do not care to tell them the truth, for they would never see it. But let the worldly man——or the frivolous woman——and then——"

At each of the pauses indicated, the mass of Shadows throbbed and heaved with emotion; but they soon settled again into comparative stillness. Once more the Shadow addressed himself to speak. But suddenly they all looked up, and the king, following their gaze, saw that the aurora had begun to pale.

"The moon is rising," said the Shadow. "As soon as she looks over the mountains into the valley, we must be gone, for we have plenty to do by the moon: we are powerful in her light. But if your majesty will come here tomorrow night, your majesty may learn a great deal more about us, and judge for himself whether it be fit to accord our petition; for then will be our grand annual assembly, in which we report to our chiefs the things we have attempted, and the good or bad success we had."

"If you send for me," returned the king, "I will come."

Ere the Shadow could reply, the tip of the moon's crescent horn peeped up from behind an icy pinnacle, and one slender ray fell on the lake. It shone upon no Shadows. Ere the eye of the king could again seek the earth after beholding the first brightness of the moon's resurrection, they had vanished; and the surface of the lake glittered cold and blue in the pale moonlight.

There the king lay, alone in the midst of the frozen lake, with the moon staring at him. But at length he heard from somewhere a voice that he knew.

"Will you take another cup of tea, dear?" said Mrs. Rinkelmann.

And Ralph, coming slowly to himself, found that he was lying in his own bed.

"Yes, I will," he answered; "and rather a large piece of toast, if you please; for I have been a long journey since I saw you last."

"He has not come to himself quite," said Mrs. Rinkelmann, between her and herself.

"You would be rather surprised," continued Ralph, "if I told you where I had been."

"I dare say I should," responded his wife.

"Then I will tell you," rejoined Ralph.

But at that moment, a great Shadow bounced out of the fire with a single huge leap, and covered the whole room. Then it settled in one corner, and Ralph saw it shaking its fist at him from the end of a preposterous arm. So he took the hint, and held his peace. And it was as well for him. For I happen to know something about the Shadows too; and I know that if he had told his wife all about it just then, they would not have sent for him the following evening.

But as the king, after finishing his tea and toast, lay and looked about him, the shadows dancing in his room seemed to him odder and more inexplicable than ever. The whole chamber was full of mystery. So it generally was, but now it was more mysterious than ever. After all that he had seen in the Shadow-church, his own room and its shadows were yet more wonderful and unintelligible than those.

This made it the more likely that he had seen a true vision; for instead of making common things look commonplace, as a false vision would have done, it had made common things disclose the wonderful that was in them.

"The same applies to all art as well," thought Ralph Rinkelmann.

The next afternoon, as the twilight was growing dusky, the king lay wondering whether or not the Shadows would fetch him again. He wanted very much to go, for he had enjoyed the journey exceedingly, and he longed, besides, to hear some of the Shadows tell their stories. But the darkness grew deeper and deeper, and the Shadows did not come. The cause was, that Mrs. Rinkelmann sat by the fire in the gloaming; and they could not carry off the king while she was there. Some of them tried to frighten her away by playing the oddest pranks on the walls, the floor, and ceiling; but altogether without effect: the queen only smiled, for she had a good conscience. Suddenly, however, a dreadful scream was heard from the nursery, and Mrs. Rinkelmann rushed up-stairs to see what was the matter. No sooner had she gone than the two warders of the chimney-corners stepped out into the middle of the room, and said, in a low voice,

"Is your majesty ready?"

"Have you no hearts?" said the king; "or are they as black as your faces? Did you not hear the child scream? I must know what is the matter with her before I go."

"Your majesty may keep his mind easy on that point," replied the warders. "We had tried everything we could think of to get rid of her majesty the queen, but without effect. So a young madcap Shadow, half against the will of the older ones of us, slipped up-stairs into the nursery; and has, no doubt, succeeded in appalling the baby, for he is very lithe and long-legged.—Now, your majesty."

"I will have no such tricks played in my nursery," said the king, rather angrily. "You might put the child beside itself."

"Then there would be twins, your majesty. And we rather like twins."

"None of your miserable jesting! You might put the child out of her wits."

"Impossible, sire; for she has not got into them yet."

"Go away," said the king.

"Forgive us, your majesty. Really, it will do the child good; for that Shadow will, all her life, be to her a symbol of what is ugly and bad. When she feels in danger of hating or envying any one, that Shadow will come back to her mind and make her shudder."

"Very well," said the king. "I like that. Let us go."

The Shadows went through the same ceremonies and preparations as before; during which, the young

Shadow before-mentioned contrived to make such grimaces as kept the baby in terror, and the queen in the nursery, till all was ready. Then with a bound that doubled him up against the ceiling, and a kick of his legs six feet out behind him, he vanished through the nursery door, and reached the king's bed-chamber just in time to take his place with the last who were melting through the window in the rear of the litter, and settling down upon the snow beneath. Away they went as before, a gliding blackness over the white carpet. And it was Christmas-eve.

When they came in sight of the mountain-lake, the king saw that it was crowded over its whole surface with a changeful intermingling of Shadows. They were all talking and listening alternately, in pairs, trios, and groups of every size. Here and there, large companies were absorbed in attention to one elevated above the rest, not in a pulpit, or on a platform, but on the stilts of his own legs, elongated for the nonce. The aurora, right overhead, lighted up the lake and the sides of the mountains, by sending down from the zenith, nearly to the surface of the lake, great folded vapours, luminous with all the colours of a faint rainbow.

Many, however, as the words were that passed on all sides, not a shadow of a sound reached the ears of the king: the shadow-speech could not enter his corporeal organs. One of his guides, however, seeing that the king wanted to hear and could not, went through a strange manipulation of his head and ears; after which he could hear perfectly, though still only the voice to which, for the time, he directed his attention. This, however, was a great advantage, and one which the king longed to carry back with him to the world of men.

The king now discovered that this was not merely the church of the Shadows, but their news-exchange at the same time. For, as the Shadows have no writing or printing, the only way in which they can make each other acquainted with their doings and thinkings, is to meet and talk at this word-mart and parliament of shades. And as, in the world, people read their favourite authors, and listen to their favourite speakers, so here the Shadows seek their favourite Shadows, listen to their adventures, and hear generally what they have to say.

Feeling quite strong, the king rose and walked about amongst them, wrapped in his ermine robe, with his red crown on his head, and his diamond sceptre in his hand. Every group of Shadows to which he drew near, ceased talking as soon as they saw him approach: but at a nod they went on again directly, conversing and relating and commenting, as if no one was there of other kind or of higher rank than themselves. So the king heard a good many stories. At some of them he laughed, and at some of them he cried. But if the stories that the Shadows told were printed, they would make a book that no publisher could produce fast enough to satisfy the buyers. I will record some of the things that the kind heard, for he told them to me soon after. In fact, I was for some time his private secretary.

"I made him confess before a week was over," said a gloomy old Shadow.

"But what was the good of that?" rejoined a pert young one. "That could not undo what was done."

"Yes, it could."

"What! bring the dead back to life?"

"No; but comfort the murderer. I could not bear to see the pitiable misery he was in. He was far happier with the rope round his neck, than he was with the purse in his pocket. I saved him from killing himself too."

"How did you make him confess?"

"Only by wallowing on the wall a little."

"How could that make him tell?"

"*He* knows."

The Shadow was silent; and the king turned to another, who was preparing to speak.

"I made a fashionable mother repent."

"How?" broke from several voices, in whose sound was mingled a touch of incredulity.

"Only by making a little coffin on the wall," was the reply.

"Did the fashionable mother confess too?"

"She had nothing more to confess than everybody knew."

"What did everybody know then?"

"That she might have been kissing a living child, when she followed a dead one to the grave.—The next will fare better."

"I put a stop to a wedding," said another.

"Horrid shade!" remarked a poetic imp.

"How?" said others. "Tell us how."

"Only by throwing a darkness, as if from the branch of a sconce, over the forehead of a fair girl.—They are not married yet, and I do not think they will be. But I loved the youth who loved her. How he started! It was a revelation to him."

"But did it not deceive him?"

"Quite the contrary."

"But it was only a shadow from the outside, not a shadow coming through from the soul of the girl."

"Yes. You may say so. But it was all that was wanted to make the meaning of her forehead manifest—yes, of her whole face, which had now and then, in the pauses of his passion, perplexed the youth. All of it, curled nostrils, pouting lips, projecting chin, instantly fell into harmony with that darkness between her eyebrows. The youth understood it in a moment, and went home miserable. And they're not married *yet*."

"I caught a toper alone, over his magnum of port," said a very dark Shadow; "and didn't I give it to him! I made *delirium tremens* first; and then I settled into a fu-neral, passing slowly along the length of the opposite wall. I gave him plenty of plumes and mourning coaches. And then I gave him a funeral service, but I could not manage to make the surplice white, which was all the better for such a sinner. The wretch stared till his face passed from purple to grey, and actually left his fifth glass only, unfinished and took refuge with his wife and children in the drawing-room, much to their surprise. I believe he actually drank a cup of tea; and although I have often looked in since, I have never caught him again, drinking alone at least."

"But does he drink less? Have you done him any good?"

"I hope so; but I am sorry to say I can't feel sure about it."

"Humph! Humph! Humph!" grunted various shadow throats.

"I had such fun once!" cried another. "I made such game of a young clergyman!"

"You have no right to make game of any one."

"Oh, yes, I have—when it is for his good. He used to study his sermons—where do you think?"

"In his study, of course. Where else should it be?"

"Yes and no. Guess again."

"Out amongst the faces in the streets?"

"Guess again."

"In still green places in the country?"

"Guess again."

"In old books?"

"Guess again."

"No, no. Tell us."

"In the looking-glass. Ha! ha! ha!"

"He was fair game; fair shadow game."

"I thought so. And I made such fun of him one night on the wall! He had sense enough to see that it was himself, and very like an ape. So he got ashamed, turned the mirror with its face to the wall, and thought a little more about his people, and a little less about himself. I was very glad; for, please your majesty,"—and here the speaker turned towards the king—"we don't like the creatures that live in the mirrors. You call them ghosts, don't you?"

Before the king could reply, another had commenced. But the story about the clergyman had made the king wish to hear one of the shadow-sermons. So he turned him towards a long Shadow, who was preaching to a very quiet and listening crowd. He was just concluding his sermon.

"Therefore, dear Shadows, it is the more needful that we love one another as much as we can, because that is not much. We have no such excuse for not loving as mortals have, for we do not die like them. I suppose it is the thought of that death that makes them hate so much. Then again, we go to sleep all day, most of us, and not in the night, as men do. And you know that we forget everything that happened the night before; therefore, we ought to love well, for the love is short. Ah! dear Shadow, whom I love now with all my shadowy soul, I shall not love thee to-morrow eve, I shall not know thee; I shall pass thee in the crowd and never dream that the Shadow whom I now love is near me then. Happy Shades! for we only remember our tales until we have told them here, and then they vanish in the shadow-churchyard, where we bury only our dead selves. Ah! brethren, who would be a man and remember? Who would be a man and weep? We ought indeed to love one another, for we alone inherit oblivion; we alone are renewed with eternal birth; we alone have no gathered weight of years.

"I will tell you the awful fate of one Shadow who rebelled against his nature, and sought to remember the past. He said, 'I *will* remember this eve.' He fought with the genial influences of kindly sleep when the sun rose on the awful dead day of light; and although he could not keep quite awake, he dreamed of the foregone eve, and he never forgot his dream. Then he tried again the next night, and the next, and the next; and he tempted another Shadow to try it with him. But at last their awful fate overtook them; for, instead of continuing to be Shadows, they began to cast shadows, as foolish men say; and so they thickened and thickened till they vanished out of our world. They are now condemned to walk the earth a man and a woman, with death behind them, and memories within them. Ah, brother Shades! let us love one another, for we shall soon forget. We are not men, but Shadows."

The king turned away, and pitied the poor Shadows far more than they pitied men.

"Oh! how we played with a musician one night," exclaimed a Shadow in another group, to which the king had first directed a passing thought, and then had stopped to listen.—"Up and down we went, like the hammers and dampers on his piano. But he took his revenge on us. For after he had watched us for half an hour in the twilight, he rose and went to his instrument and played a shadow-dance that fixed us all in sound for ever. Each could tell the very notes meant for him; and as long as he played we could not stop, but went on dancing and dancing after the music, just as the magician—I mean the musician—pleased.

"And he punished us well; for he nearly danced us all off our legs and out of shape into tired heaps of collapsed and palpitating darkness. We won't go near him for some time again, if we can only remember it. He had been very miserable all day, he was so poor; and we could not think of any way of comforting him except making him laugh. We did not succeed, with our wildest efforts; but it turned out better than we had expected, after all; for his shadow-dance got him into notice, and he is quite popular now, making money fast. If he does not take care, we shall have other work to do with him by-and-by, poor fellow!"

"I and some others did the same for a poor playwriter once. He had a Christmas piece to write, and being an original genius, it was not so easy for him to find a subject as it is for most of his class. I saw the trouble he was in, and collecting a few stray Shadows, we acted, in dumb show of course, the funniest bit of nonsense we could think of; and it was quite successful. The poor fellow watched every motion, roaring with laughter at us, and delight at the ideas we put into his head. He turned it all into words, and scenes, and actions; and the piece came off with a splendid success."

"But how long we have to look for a chance of doing anything worth doing!" said a long, thin, especially lugubrious Shadow. "I have only done one thing worth telling ever since we met last. But I am proud of that."

"What was it? What was it?" rose from twenty voices.

"I crept into a dining-room, one twilight, soon after Christmas-day. I had been drawn thither by the glow of a bright fire shining through red window-curtains. At first I thought there was no one there, and was on the point of leaving the room and going out again into the snowy street, when I suddenly caught the sparkle of eyes. I found that they belonged to a little boy who lay very still on a sofa. I crept into a dark corner by the sideboard, and watched him. He seemed very sad, and did nothing but stare into the fire.

"At last he sighed out,—'I wish mamma would come home.' 'Poor boy!' thought I, 'there is no help for that but mamma.' Yet I would try to while away the time for him. So out of my corner I stretched a long shadow arm, reaching all across the ceiling, and pretended to make a grab at him. He was rather frightened at first; but he was

112

a brave boy, and soon saw that it was all a joke. So when I did it again, he made a clutch at me; and then we had such fun! For though he often sighed and wished mamma would come home, he always began again with me; and on we went with the wildest game.

"At last his mother's knock came to the door, and, starting up in delight, he rushed into the hall to meet her, and forgot all about poor black me. But I did not mind that in the least; for when I glided out after him into the hall, I was well repaid for my trouble by hearing his mother say to him,—'Why, Charlie, my dear, you look ever so much better since I left you!' At that moment I slipped through the closing door, and as I ran across the snow, I heard the mother say,—'What Shadow can that be passing so quickly?' And Charlie answered with a merry laugh,—'Oh! mamma, I suppose it must be the funny Shadow that has been playing such games with me all the time you were out.' As soon as the door was shut, I crept along the wall and looked in at the dining-room window. And I heard his mamma say, as she led him into the room,—'What an imagination the boy has!' Ha! ha! ha! Then she looked at him, and the tears came in her eyes; and she stooped down over him, and I heard the sounds of a mingling kiss and sob."

"I always look for nurseries full of children," said another; "and this winter I have been very fortunate. I am sure children belong especially to us. One evening, looking about in a great city, I saw through the window into a large nursery, where the odious gas had not yet been lighted. Round the fire sat a company of the most delightful children I have ever seen. They were waiting patiently for their tea. It was too good an opportunity to be lost. I hurried away, and gathering together twenty of the best Shadows I could find, returned in a few moments; and entering the nursery, we danced on the walls one of our best dances. To be sure it was mostly extemporized; but I managed to keep it in harmony by singing this song which I made as we went on. Of course the children could not hear it: they only saw the motions that answered to it; but with them they seemed to be very much delighted indeed, as I shall presently prove to you. This was the song:—

Swing, swang, swingle, swuff!
Flicker, flacker, fling, fluff!
 Thus we go,
 To and fro;
 Here and there,
 Everywhere,
 Born and bred;
 Never dead,
  Only gone.

  On! Come on.
 Looming, glooming,
 Spreading, fuming,
 Shattering, scattering,
 Parting, darting,
 Settling, starting,
 All our life
 Is a strife,
And a wearying for rest
On the darkness' friendly breast
 Joining, splitting,
 Rising, sitting,
 Laughing, shaking,
 Sides all aching,
Grumbling, grim, and gruff.
Swingle, swangle, swuff!
 Now a knot of darkness;
  Now dissolved gloom;
 Now a pall of blackness
  Hiding all the room.
Flicker, flacker, fluff!
Black, and black enough!

Dancing now like demons;
　Lying like the dead;
Gladly would we stop it,
　And go down to bed!
But our work we still must do,
Shadow men, as well as you.

Rooting, rising, shooting,
　Heaving, sinking, creeping;
Hid in corners crooning;
　Splitting, poking, leaping,
Gathering, towering, swooning.
　When we're lurking,
　Yet we're working,
For our labour we must do,
Shadow men, as well as you.
　Flicker, flacker, fling, fluff!
　Swing, swang, swingle, swuff!

" 'How thick the Shadows are!' said one of the children—a thoughtful little girl.

" 'I wonder where they come from,' said a dreamy little boy.

" 'I think they grow out of the wall,' answered the little girl; 'for I have been watching them come; first one, and then another, and then a whole lot of them. I am sure they grow out of the walls.'

" 'Perhaps they have papas and mammas,' said an older boy, with a smile.

" 'Yes, yes; and the doctor brings them in his pocket,' said another, a consequential little maiden.

" 'No; I'll tell you,' said the older boy; 'they're ghosts.'

" 'But ghosts are white.'

" 'Oh! but these have got black coming down the chimney.'

" 'No,' said a curious-looking, white-faced boy of fourteen, who had been reading by the firelight, and had stopped to hear the little ones talk; 'they're body ghosts; they're not soul ghosts.'

"A silence followed, broken by the first, the dreamy-eyed boy, who said,—

" 'I hope they didn't make me;' at which they all burst out laughing.

"Just then the nurse brought in their tea, and when she proceeded to light the gas we vanished."

"I stopped a murder," cried another.

"How? How? How?"

"I will tell you. I had been lurking about a sick room for some time, where a miser lay, apparently dying. I did not like the place at all, but I felt as if I should be wanted there. There were plenty of lurking-places about, for the room was full of all sorts of old furniture, especially cabinets, chests, and presses. I believe he had in that room every bit of the property he had spent a long life in gathering. I found that he had gold and gold in those places; for one night, when his nurse was away, he crept out of bed, mumbling and shaking, and managed to open one of the chests, though he nearly fell down with the effort. I was peeping over his shoulder, and such a gleam of gold fell upon me, that it nearly killed me. But hearing his nurse coming, he slammed the lid down, and I recovered.

"I tried very hard, but I could not do him any good. For although I made all sorts of shapes on the walls and ceilings, representing evil deeds that he had done, of which there were plenty to choose from, I could make no shapes on his brain or conscience. He had no eyes for anything but gold. And it so happened that his nurse had neither eyes nor heart for anything else either.

"One day, as she was seated beside his bed, but where he could not see her, stirring some gruel in a basin, to cool it for him, I saw her take a little phial from her bosom, and I knew by the expression of her face both what it was and what she was going to do with it. Fortunately the cork was a little hard to get out, and this gave me one moment to think.

"The room was so crowded with all sorts of things, that although there were no curtains on the four-post bed to hide from the miser the sight of his precious treasures, there was yet but one small part of the ceiling suitable for casting myself upon in the shape I wished to assume. And this spot was hard to reach. But having discovered that upon this very place lay a dull gleam of firelight thrown from a strange old dusty mirror that stood away in some corner, I got in front of the fire, spied where the mirror was, threw myself upon it, and bounded from its face upon the oval pool of dim light on the ceiling, assuming, as I passed, the shape of an old stooping hag, who poured something from a phial into a basin. I made the handle of the spoon with my own nose, ha! ha!"

And the shadow-hand caressed the shadow-tip of the shadow-nose, before the shadow-tongue resumed.

"The old miser saw me: he would not taste the gruel that night, although his nurse coaxed and scolded till they were both weary. She pretended to taste it herself, and to think it very good; but at last retired into a corner, and after making as if she were eating it, took good care to pour it all out into the ashes."

"But she must either succeed, or starve him, at last," interposed a Shadow.

"I will tell you."

"And," interposed another, "he was not worth saving."

"He might repent," suggested a third, who was more benevolent.

"No chance of that," returned the former. "Misers never do. The love of money has less in it to cure itself than any other wickedness into which wretched men can fall. What a mercy it is to be born a Shadow! Wickedness does not stick to us. What do we care for gold!— Rubbish!"

"Amen! Amen! Amen!" came from a hundred shadow-voices.

"You should have let her murder him, and so you would have been quit of him."

"And besides how was he to escape at last? He could never get rid of her, you know."

"I was going to tell you," resumed the narrator, "only you had so many shadow-remarks to make, that you would not let me."

"Go on; go on."

"There was a little grandchild who used to come and see him sometimes—the only creature the miser cared for. Her mother was his daughter; but the old man would never see her, because she had married against his will. Her husband was now dead, but he had not forgiven her yet. After the shadow he had seen, however, he said to himself, as he lay awake that night—I saw the words on his face—'How shall I get rid of that old devil? If I don't eat I shall die; and if I do eat I shall be poisoned. I wish little Mary would come. Ah! her mother would never have served me so.' He lay awake, thinking such things over and over again, all night long, and I stood watching him from a dark corner, till the dayspring came and shook me out. When I came back the next night, the room was tidy and clean. His own daughter, a sadfaced but beautiful woman, sat by his bedside; and little Mary was curled up on the floor by the fire, imitating us, by making queer shadows on the ceiling with her twisted hands. But she could not think however they got there. And no wonder, for I helped her to some very unaccountable ones."

"I have a story about a granddaughter, too," said another, the moment that speaker ceased.

"Tell it. Tell it."

"Last Christmas-day," he began, "I and a troop of us set out in the twilight to find some house where we could all have something to do; for we had made up our minds to act together. We tried several, but found objections to them all. At last we espied a large lonely country-house, and hastening to it, we found great preparations making for the Christmas dinner. We rushed into it, scampered all over it, and made up our minds in a moment that it would do. We amused ourselves in the nursery first, where there were several children being dressed for dinner. We generally do go to the nursery first, your majesty. This time we were especially charmed with a little girl about five years old, who clapped her hands and danced about with delight at the antics we performed; and we said we would do something for her if we had a chance.

"The company began to arrive; and at every arrival, we rushed to the hall, and cut wonderful capers of welcome. Between times, we scudded away to see how the dressing went on. One girl about eighteen was delightful. She dressed herself as if she did not care much about it, but could not help doing it prettily. When she took her last look at the phantom in the glass, she half smiled to it.—But *we* do not like those creatures that come into the mirrors at all, your majesty. We don't understand them. They are dreadful to us.—She looked rather sad and pale, but very sweet and hopeful. So we wanted to know all about her, and soon found out that she was a distant relation and a great favourite of the gentleman of the house, an old man, in whose face benevolence was mingled with obstinacy and a deep shade of the tyrannical. We could not admire him much; but we would not make up our minds all at once: Shadows never do.

"The dinner-bell rang, and down we hurried. The children all looked happy, and we were merry. But there was one cross fellow among the servants, and didn't we plague him! and didn't we get fun out of him! When he was bringing up dishes, we lay in wait for him at every corner, and sprang upon him from the floor, and from over the banisters, and down from the cornices. He started and stumbled and blundered so in consequence, that his fellow-servants thought he was tipsy. Once he dropped a plate, and had to pick up the pieces, and hurry away with them; and didn't we pursue him as he went! It was lucky for him his master did not see how he went on; but we took care not to let him get into any real scrape, though he was quite dazed with the dodging of the unaccountable shadows. Sometimes he thought the walls were coming down upon him, sometimes that the floor was gaping to swallow him; sometimes that he would be knocked to pieces by the hurrying to and fro, or be smothered in the black crowd.

"When the blazing plum-pudding was carried in, we made a perfect shadow-carnival about it, dancing and mumming in the blue flames, like mad demons. And how the children screamed with delight!

"The old gentleman, who was very fond of children, was laughing his heartiest laugh, when a loud knock came to the hall-door. The fair maiden started, turned paler, and then red as the Christmas fire. I saw it, and flung my hands across her face. She was very glad, and I know she said in her heart, 'You kind Shadow!' which paid me well. Then I followed the rest into the hall, and found there a jolly, handsome, brown-faced sailor, evidently a son of the house. The old man received him with tears in his eyes, and the children with shouts of joy. The maiden escaped in the confusion, just in time to save herself from fainting. We crowded about the lamp to hide her retreat, and nearly put it out; and the butler could not get it to burn up before she had glided into her place again, relieved to find the room so dark. The sailor only had seen her go, and now he sat down beside her, and, without a word, got hold of her hand in the gloom. When we all scattered to the walls and the corners, and the lamp blazed up again, he let her hand go.

"During the rest of the dinner the old man watched the two, and saw that there was something between them, and was very angry. For he was an important man in his own estimation, and they had never consulted him. The fact was, they had never known their own minds till the sailor had gone upon his last voyage, and had learned each other's only this moment.—We found out all this by watching them, and then talking together about it afterwards.—The old gentleman saw, too, that his favourite, who was under such obligation to him for loving her so much, loved his son better than him; and he grew by degrees so jealous that he overshadowed the whole table with his morose looks and short answers. That kind of shadowing is very different from ours; and the Christmas dessert grew so gloomy that we Shadows could not bear it, and were delighted when the ladies rose to go to the drawing-room. The gentlemen would not stay behind the ladies, even for the sake of the well-known wine.

"So the moody host, notwithstanding his hospitality, was left alone at the table in the great silent room. We followed the company up-stairs to the drawing-room, and thence to the nursery for snap-dragon; but while they were busy with this most shadowy of games, nearly all the Shadows crept down-stairs again to the dining-room, where the old man still sat, gnawing the bone of his own selfishness. They crowded into the room, and by using every kind of expansion—blowing themselves out like soap bubbles—they succeeded in heaping up the whole room with shade upon shade. They clustered thickest about the fire and the lamp, till at last they almost drowned them in hills of darkness.

"Before they had accomplished so much, the children, tired with fun and frolic, had been put to bed. But the little girl of five years old, with whom we had been so pleased when first we arrived, could not go to sleep. She had a little room of her own; and I had watched her to bed, and now kept her awake by gambolling in the rays of the night-light. When her eyes were once fixed upon me, I took the shape of her grandfather, representing him on the wall as he sat in his chair, with his head bent down and his arms hanging listlessly by his sides. And the child remembered that that was just as she had seen him last; for she had happened to peep in at the dining-room door after all the rest had gone up-stairs. 'What if he should be sitting there still,' thought she, 'all alone in the dark!' She scrambled out of bed and crept down.

"Meantime the others had made the room below so dark, that only the face and white hair of the old man could be dimly discerned in the shadowy crowd. For he had filled his own mind with shadows, which we Shadows wanted to draw out of him. Those shadows are very different from us, your majesty knows. He was thinking of all the disappointments he had had in life, and of all the ingratitude he had met with. And he thought far more of the good he had done, than the good others had got. 'After all I have done for them,' said he, with a sigh of bitterness, 'not one of them cares a straw for me. My own children will be glad when I am gone!'

"At that instant he lifted up his eyes and saw, standing close by the door, a tiny figure in a long nightgown. The door behind her was shut. It was my little friend, who had crept in noiselessly. A pang of icy fear shot to the old man's heart, but it melted away as fast, for we made a lane through us for a single ray from the fire to fall on the face of the little sprite; and he thought it was a child of his own that had died when just the age of her child-niece, who now stood looking for her grandfather among the Shadows. He thought she had come out of her grave in the cold darkness to ask why her father was sitting along on Christmas-day. And he felt he had no answer to give his little ghost, but one he would be ashamed for her to hear. But his grandchild saw him now, and walked up to him with a childish stateliness, stumbling once or twice on what seemed her long shroud. Pushing through the crowded shadows, she reached him, climbed upon his knee, laid her little long-haired head on his shoulders, and said,—'Ganpa! you goomy? Isn't it your Kissy-Day too, ganpa?'

"A new fount of love seemed to burst from the clay of the old man's heart. He clasped the child to his bosom, and wept. Then, without a word, he rose with her in his arms, carried her up to her room, and laying her down in her bed, covered her up, kissed her sweet little mouth unconscious of reproof, and then went to the drawing-room.

"As soon as he entered, he saw the culprits in a quiet corner alone. He went up to them, took a hand of each, and joining them in both his, said, 'God bless you!' Then he turned to the rest of the company, and 'Now,' said he, 'let's have a Christmas carol.'—And well we might; for though I have paid many visits to the house, I have never seen him cross since; and I am sure that must cost him a good deal of trouble."

"We have just come from a great palace," said another, "where we knew there were many children, and where we thought to hear glad voices, and see royally merry looks. But as soon as we entered, we became aware that one mighty Shadow shrouded the whole; and that Shadow deepened and deepened, till it gathered in darkness about the reposing form of a wise prince. When we saw him, we could move no more, but clung heavily to the walls, and by our stillness added to the sorrow of the hour. And when we saw the mother of her people weeping with bowed head for the loss of him in whom she had trusted, we were seized with such a longing to be Shadows no more, but winged angels, which are the white shadows cast in heaven from the Light of Light, so as to gather around her, and hover over her with comforting, that we vanished from the walls, and found ourselves floating high above the towers of the palace, where we met the angels on their way, and knew that our service was not needed."

By this time there was a glimmer of approaching moonlight, and the king began to see several of those stranger Shadows, with human faces and eyes, moving about amongst the crowd. He knew at once that they did not belong to his dominion. They looked at him, and came near him, and passed slowly, but they never made any obeisance, or gave sign of homage. And what their eyes said to him, the king only could tell. And he did not tell.

"What are those other Shadows that move through the crowd?" said he to one of his subjects near him.

The Shadow started, looked around, shivered slightly, and laid his finger on his lips. Then leading the king a little aside, and looking carefully about him once more,—

"I do not know," said he, in a low tone, "what they are. I have heard of them often, but only once did I ever see any of them before. That was when some of us one night paid a visit to a man who sat much alone, and was said to think a great deal. We saw two of those sitting in the room with him, and he was as pale as they were. We could not cross the threshold, but shivered and shook, and felt ready to melt away. Is not your majesty afraid of them too!"

But the king made no answer; and before he could speak again, the moon had climbed above the mighty pillars of the church of the Shadows, and looked in at the great window of the sky.

The shapes had all vanished; and the king, again lifting up his eyes, saw but the walls of his own chamber, on which flickered the Shadow of a Little Child. He looked down, and there, sitting on a stool by the fire, he saw one of his own little ones, waiting to say good night to his father, and go to bed early, that he might rise early too, and be very good and happy all Christmas-day.

And Ralph Rinkelmann rejoiced that he was a man, and not a Shadow.

But as the Shadows vanished they left the sense of song in the king's brain. And the words of their song must have been something like these:—

> Shadows, Shadows, Shadows all!
> Shadow birth and funeral!
> Shadow moons gleam overhead;
> Over shadow graves we tread.
> Shadow-hope lives, grows, and dies
> Shadow-love from Shadow-eyes
> Shadow-ward entices on
> To shadow-words on shadow-stone,
> Closing up the shadow-tale
> With a shadow-shadow-wail.
>
> Shadow-man, thou art a gloom
> Cast upon a shadow-tomb
> Through the endless shadow-air,
> From the Shadow sitting there,
> On a moveless shadow-throne,
> Glooming through the ages gone
> North and south, in and out,
> East and west, and all about,
> Flinging Shadows everywhere
> On the Shadow-painted air.
> Shadow-man, thou hast no story,
> Nothing but a shadow-glory.

But Ralph Rinkelmann said to himself,—

"They are but Shadows that sing thus; for a Shadow can see but Shadows. A man sees a man where a Shadow sees only a Shadow."

And he was comforted in himself.

"The Golden Key" appeared *in* Dealings with the Fairies, *which was published in 1867, and is also considered one of MacDonald's finest fairy tales. The story involves a boy who finds a golden key at the bottom of a rainbow and sets out in search of the one lock it will open. What he discovers is Fairyland, a place that lies above earth and is intermediate between our present dwelling place and our ultimate home. Fairyland is a higher world, one of glory and wonder, and MacDonald uses it to express his belief that as creation grows in spiritual wisdom it also becomes freer and more beautiful.*

∾

CHAPTER FOUR

The Golden Key

There was a boy who used to sit in the twilight and listen to his great-aunt's stories.

She told him that if he could reach the place where the end of the rainbow stands he would find there a golden key.

"And what is the key for?" the boy would ask. "What is it the key of? What will it open?"

"That nobody knows," his aunt would reply. "He has to find that out."

"I suppose, being gold," the boy once said, thoughtfully, "that I could get a good deal of money for it if I sold it."

"Better never find it than sell it," returned his aunt.

And then the boy went to bed and dreamed about the golden key.

Now all that his great-aunt told the boy about the golden key would have been nonsense, had it not been that their little house stood on the borders of Fairyland. For it is perfectly well known that out of Fairyland nobody ever can find where the rainbow stands. The creature takes such good care of its golden key, always flitting from place to place, lest any one should find it! But in Fairyland it is quite different. Things that look real in this country look very thin indeed in Fairyland, while some of the things that here cannot stand still for a moment, will not move there. So it was not in the least absurd of the old lady to tell her nephew such things about the golden key.

"Did you ever know anybody to find it?" he asked, one evening.

"Yes. Your father, I believe, found it."

"And what did he do with it, can you tell me?"

"He never told me."

"What was it like?"

"He never showed it to me."

"How does a new key come there always?"

"I don't know. There it is."

"Perhaps it is the rainbow's egg."

"Perhaps it is. You will be a happy boy if you find the nest."

"Perhaps it comes tumbling down the rainbow from the sky."

"Perhaps it does."

One evening, in summer, he went into his own room, and stood at the lattice-window, and gazed into the forest which fringed the outskirts of Fairyland. It came close up to his great-aunt's garden, and, indeed, sent some straggling trees into it. The forest lay to the east, and the sun, which was setting behind the cottage, looked straight into the dark wood with his level red eye. The trees were all old, and had few branches below, so that the sun could see a great way into the forest; and the boy, being keen-sighted, could see almost as far as the sun. The trunks stood like rows of red columns in the shine of the red sun, and he could see down aisle after aisle in the vanishing distance. And as he gazed into the forest he began to feel as if the trees were all waiting for him, and had something they could not go on with till he came to them. But he was hungry, and wanted his supper. So he lingered.

Suddenly, far among the trees, as far as the sun could shine, he saw a glorious thing. It was the end of a rainbow, large and brilliant. He could count all the seven colours, and could see shade after shade beyond the violet; while before the red stood a colour more gorgeous and mysterious still. It was a colour he had never seen before. Only the spring of the rainbow-arch was visible. He could see nothing of it above the trees.

"The golden key!" he said to himself, and darted out of the house, and into the wood.

He had not gone far before the sun set. But the rainbow only glowed the brighter. For the rainbow of Fairyland is not dependent upon the sun as ours is. The trees welcomed him. The bushes made way for him. The rainbow grew larger and brighter; and at length he found himself within two trees of it.

It was a grand sight, burning away there in silence, with its gorgeous, its lovely, its delicate colours, each distinct, all combining. He could now see a great deal more of it. It rose high into the blue heavens, but bent so little that he could not tell how high the crown of the arch must reach. It was still only a small portion of a huge bow.

He stood gazing at it till he forgot himself with delight—even forgot the key which he had come to seek. And as he stood it grew more wonderful still. For in each of the colours, which was as large as the column of a church, he could faintly see beautiful forms slowly ascending as if by the steps of a winding stair. The forms appeared irregularly—now one, now many, now several, now none—men and women and children—all different, all beautiful.

He drew nearer to the rainbow. It vanished. He started

back a step in dismay. It was there again, as beautiful as ever. So he contented himself with standing as near it as he might, and watching the forms that ascended the glorious colours towards the unknown height of the arch, which did not end abruptly, but faded away in the blue air, so gradually that he could not say where it ceased.

When the thought of the golden key returned, the boy very wisely proceeded to mark out in his mind the space covered by the foundation of the rainbow, in order that he might know where to search, should the rainbow disappear. It was based chiefly upon a bed of moss.

Meantime it had grown quite dark in the wood. The rainbow alone was visible by its own light. But the moment the moon rose the rainbow vanished. Nor could any change of place restore the vision to the boy's eyes. So he threw himself down on the mossy bed, to wait till the sunlight would give him a chance of finding the key. There he fell fast asleep.

When he awoke in the morning the sun was looking straight into his eyes. He turned away from it, and the same moment saw a brilliant little thing lying on the moss within a foot of his face. It was the golden key. The pipe of it was of plain gold, as bright as gold could be. The handle was curiously wrought and set with sapphires. In a terror of delight he put out his hand and took it, and had it.

He lay for a while, turning it over and over, and feeding his eyes upon its beauty. Then he jumped to his feet, remembering that the pretty thing was of no use to him yet. Where was the lock to which the key belonged? It must be somewhere, for how could anybody be so silly as make a key for which there was no lock? Where should he go to look for it? He gazed about him, up into the air, down to the earth, but saw no keyhole in the clouds, in the grass, or in the trees.

Just as he began to grow disconsolate, however, he saw

something glimmering in the wood. It was a mere glimmer that he saw, but he took it for a glimmer of rainbow, and went towards it.—And now I will go back to the borders of the forest.

Not far from the house where the boy had lived, there was another house, the owner of which was a merchant, who was much away from home. He had lost his wife some years before, and had only one child, a little girl, whom he left to the charge of two servants, who were very idle and careless. So she was neglected and left untidy, and was sometimes ill-used besides.

Now it is well known that the little creatures commonly called fairies, though there are many different kinds of fairies in Fairyland, have an exceeding dislike to untidiness. Indeed, they are quite spiteful to slovenly people. Being used to all the lovely ways of the trees and flowers, and to the neatness of the birds and all woodland creatures, it makes them feel miserable, even in their deep woods and on their grassy carpets to think that within the same moonlight lies a dirty, uncomfortable, slovenly house. And this makes them angry with the people that live in it, and they would gladly drive them out of the world if they could. They want the whole earth nice and clean. So they pinch the maids black and blue, and play them all manner of uncomfortable tricks.

But this house was quite a shame, and the fairies in the forest could not endure it. They tried everything on the maids without effect, and at last resolved upon making a clean riddance, beginning with the child. They ought to have known that it was not her fault, but they have little principle and much mischief in them, and they thought that if they got rid of her the maids would be sure to be turned away.

So one evening, the poor little girl having been put to bed early, before the sun was down, the servants went off to the village, locking the door behind them. The child did not know she was alone, and lay contentedly looking out of her window towards the forest, of which, however, she could not see much, because of the ivy and other creeping plants which had straggled across her window. All at once she saw an ape making faces at her out of the mirror, and the heads carved upon a great old wardrobe grinning fearfully. Then two old spider-legged chairs came forward into the middle of the room, and began to dance a queer, old-fashioned dance. This set her laughing, and she forgot the ape and the grinning heads.

So the fairies saw they had made a mistake, and sent the chairs back to their places. But they knew that she had been reading the story of Silverhair all day. So the next moment she heard the voices of the three bears upon the stair, big voice, middle voice, and little voice, and she heard their soft, heavy tread, as if they had had stockings over their boots, coming nearer and nearer to the door of her room, till she could bear it no longer. She did just as Silverhair did, and as the fairies wanted her to do: she darted to the window, pulled it open, got upon the ivy, and so scrambled to the ground. She then fled to the forest as fast as she could run.

Now, although she did not know it, this was the very best way she could have gone; for nothing is ever so mischievous in its own place as it is out of it; and, besides, these mischievous creatures were only the children of Fairyland, as it were, and there are many other beings there as well; and if a wanderer gets in among them, the good ones will always help him more than the evil ones will be able to hurt him.

The sun was now set, and the darkness coming on, but the child thought of no danger but the bears behind her. If she had looked round, however, she would have seen that she was followed by a very different creature from a bear. It was a curious creature, made like a fish, but covered, instead of scales, with feathers of all colours, sparkling like those of a humming-bird. It had fins, not wings, and swam through the air as a fish does through the water. Its head was like the head of a small owl.

After running a long way, and as the last of the light was disappearing, she passed under a tree with drooping branches. It propped its branches to the ground all about her, and caught her as in a trap. She struggled to get out, but the branches pressed her closer and closer to the trunk. She was in great terror and distress, when the air-fish, swimming into the thicket of branches, began tearing them with its beak. They loosened their hold at once, and the creature went on attacking them, till at length they let the child go. Then the air-fish came from behind her, and swam on in front, glittering and sparkling all lovely colours; and she followed.

It led her gently along till all at once it swam in at a cottage-door. The child followed still. There was a bright fire in the middle of the floor, upon which stood a pot without a lid, full of water that boiled and bubbled furiously. The air-fish swam straight to the pot and into the boiling water, where it lay quiet. A beautiful woman rose from the opposite side of the fire and came to meet the girl. She took her up in her arms, and said,—

"Ah, you are come at last! I have been looking for you a long time."

She sat down with her on her lap, and there the girl sat staring at her. She had never seen anything so beautiful. She was tall and strong, with white arms and neck, and a delicate flush on her face. The child could not tell what was the colour of her hair, but could not help thinking it had a tinge of dark green. She had not one ornament upon her, but she looked as if she had just put off quantities of diamonds and emeralds. Yet here she was in the simplest, poorest little cottage, where she was evidently at home. She was dressed in shining green.

The girl looked at the lady, and the lady looked at the girl.

"What is your name?" asked the lady.

135

"The servants always called me Tangle."

"Ah, that was because your hair was so untidy. But that was their fault, the naughty women! Still it is a pretty name, and I will call you Tangle too. You must not mind my asking you questions, for you may ask me the same questions, every one of them, and any others that you like. How old are you?"

"Ten," answered Tangle.

"You don't look like it," said the lady.

"How old are you, please?" returned Tangle.

"Thousands of years old," answered the lady.

"You don't look like it," said Tangle.

"Don't I? I think I do. Don't you see how beautiful I am?"

And her great blue eyes looked down on the little Tangle, as if all the stars in the sky were melted in them to make their brightness.

"Ah! but," said Tangle, "when people live long they grow old. At least I always thought so."

"I have no time to grow old," said the lady. "I am too busy for that. It is very idle to grow old.—But I cannot have my little girl so untidy. Do you know I can't find a clean spot on your face to kiss?"

"Perhaps," suggested Tangle, feeling ashamed, but not too much so to say a word for herself—"perhaps that is because the tree made me cry so."

"My poor darling!" said the lady, looking now as if the moon were melted in her eyes, and kissing her little face, dirty as it was, "the naughty tree must suffer for making a girl cry."

"And what is your name, please?" asked Tangle.

"Grandmother," answered the lady.

"Is it, really?"

"Yes, indeed. I never tell stories, even in fun.

"How good of you!"

"I couldn't if I tried. It would come true if I said it, and then I should be punished enough."

And she smiled like the sun through a summer-shower.

"But now," she went on, "I must get you washed and dressed, and then we shall have some supper."

"Oh! I had supper long ago," said Tangle.

"Yes, indeed you had," answered the lady—"three years ago. You don't know that it is three years since you ran away from the bears. You are thirteen and more now."

Tangle could only stare. She felt quite sure it was true.

"You will not be afraid of anything I do with you—will you?" said the lady.

"I will try very hard not to be; but I can't be certain, you know," replied Tangle.

"I like your saying so, and I shall be quite satisfied," answered the lady.

She took off the girl's night-gown, rose with her in her arms, and going to the wall of the cottage, opened a door. Then Tangle saw a deep tank, the sides of which were filled with green plants, which had flowers of all colours. There was a roof over it like the roof of the cottage. It was filled with beautiful clear water, in which swam a multitude of such fishes as the one that had led her to the cottage. It was the light their colours gave that showed the place in which they were.

The lady spoke some words Tangle could not understand, and threw her into the tank.

The fishes came crowding about her. Two or three of them got under her head and kept it up. The rest of them rubbed themselves all over her, and with their wet feathers washed her quite clean. Then the lady, who had been looking on all the time, spoke again; whereupon some thirty or forty of the fishes rose out of the water underneath Tangle, and so bore her up to the arms the lady held out to take her. She carried her back to the fire, and, having dried her well, opened a chest, and taking out the finest linen garments, smelling of grass and lavender, put them upon her, and over all a green dress, just like her own, shining like hers, and soft like hers, and going into just such lovely folds from the waist, where it was tied with a brown cord, to her bare feet.

"Won't you give me a pair of shoes too, grandmother?" said Tangle.

"No, my dear; no shoes. Look here. I wear no shoes."

So saying, she lifted her dress a little, and there were the loveliest white feet, but no shoes. Then Tangle was content to go without shoes too. And the lady sat down with her again, and combed her hair, and brushed it, and then left it to dry while she got the supper.

First she got bread out of one hole in the wall; then milk out of another; then several kinds of fruit out of a third; and then she went to the pot on the fire, and took out the fish now nicely cooked, and, as soon as she had pulled off its feathered skin, ready to be eaten.

"But," exclaimed Tangle. And she stared at the fish, and could say no more.

"I know what you mean," returned the lady. "You do not like to eat the messenger that brought you home. But it is the kindest return you can make. The creature was afraid to go until it saw me put the pot on, and heard me promise it should be boiled the moment it returned with you. Then it darted out of the door at once. You saw it go into the pot of itself the moment it entered, did you not?"

"I did," answered Tangle, "and I thought it very strange; but then I saw you, and forgot all about the fish."

"In Fairyland," resumed the lady, as they sat down to the table, "the ambition of the animals is to be eaten by the people; for that is their highest end in that condition. But they are not therefore destroyed. Out of that pot comes something more than the dead fish, you will see."

Tangle now remarked that the lid was on the pot. But the lady took no further notice of it till they had eaten the fish, which Tangle found nicer than any fish she had ever tasted before. It was as white as snow, and as delicate as cream. And the moment she had swallowed a mouthful of it, a change she could not describe began to take place in her. She heard a murmuring all about her, which became more and more articulate, and at length, as she went on eating, grew intelligible. By the time she had finished her share, the sounds of all the animals in the forest came crowding through the door to her ears; for the door still stood wide open, though it was pitch dark outside; and they were no longer sounds only; they were speech, and speech that she could understand. She could tell what the insects in the cottage were saying to each other too. She had even a suspicion that the trees and flowers all about the cottage were holding midnight communications with each other; but what they said she could not hear.

As soon as the fish was eaten, the lady went to the fire and took the lid off the pot. A lovely little creature in human shape, with large white wings, rose out of it, and flew round and round the roof of the cottage; then dropped, fluttering, and nestled in the lap of the lady. She spoke to it some strange words, carried it to the door, and threw it out into the darkness. Tangle heard the flapping of its wings die away in the distance.

"Now have we done the fish any harm?" she said, returning.

"No," answered Tangle, "I do not think we have. I should not mind eating one every day."

"They must wait their time, like you and me too, my little Tangle."

And she smiled a smile which the sadness in it made more lovely.

"But," she continued, "I think we may have one for supper to-morrow."

So saying she went to the door of the tank, and spoke; and now Tangle understood her perfectly.

"I want one of you," she said,—"the wisest."

Thereupon the fishes got together in the middle of the tank, with their heads forming a circle above the water, and their tails a larger circle beneath it. They were holding a council, in which their relative wisdom should be determined. At length one of them flew up into the lady's hand, looking lively and ready.

"You know where the rainbow stands?" she asked.

"Yes, mother, quite well," answered the fish.

"Bring home a young man you will find there, who does not know where to go."

The fish was out of the door in a moment. Then the lady told Tangle it was time to go to bed; and, opening another door in the side of the cottage, showed her a little arbour, cool and green, with a bed of purple heath growing in it, upon which she threw a large wrapper made of the feathered skins of the wise fishes, shining gorgeous in the firelight. Tangle was soon lost in the strangest, loveliest dreams. And the beautiful lady was in every one of her dreams.

In the morning she woke to the rustling of leaves over her head, and the sound of running water. But, to her surprise, she could find no door—nothing but the moss-grown wall of the cottage. So she crept through an opening in the arbour, and stood in the forest. Then she bathed in a stream that ran merrily through the trees, and felt happier; for having once been in her grandmother's pond, she must be clean and tidy ever after; and, having put on her green dress, felt like a lady.

She spent that day in the wood, listening to the birds and beasts and creeping things. She understood all that they said, though she could not repeat a word of it; and every kind had a different language, while there was a common though more limited understanding between all the inhabitants of the forest. She saw nothing of the beautiful lady, but she felt that she was near her all the time; and she took care not to go out of sight of the cottage. It was round, like a snow-hut or a wigwam; and she could see neither door nor window in it. The fact was, it had no windows; and though it was full of doors, they all opened from the inside, and could not even be seen from the outside.

She was standing at the foot of a tree in the twilight, listening to a quarrel between a mole and a squirrel, in which the mole told the squirrel that the tail was the best of him, and the squirrel called the mole Spade-fists, when, the darkness having deepened around her, she became aware of something shining in her face, and looking round, saw that the door of the cottage was open, and the red light of the fire flowing from it like a river through the darkness. She left Mole and Squirrel to settle matters as they might, and darted off to the cottage. Entering, she found the pot boiling on the fire, and the grand, lovely lady sitting on the other side of it.

"I've been watching you all day," said the lady. "You shall have something to eat by-and-by, but we must wait till our supper comes home."

She took Tangle on her knee, and began to sing to her—such songs as made her wish she could listen to them for ever. But at length in rushed the shining fish, and snuggled down in the pot. It was followed by a youth who had outgrown his worn garments. His face was ruddy with health, and in his hand he carried a little jewel, which sparkled in the firelight.

The first words the lady said were,—

"What is that in your hand, Mossy?"

Now Mossy was the name his companions had given him, because he had a favourite stone covered with moss, on which he used to sit whole days reading; and they said the moss had begun to grow upon him too.

Mossy held out his hand. The moment the lady saw that it was the golden key, she rose from her chair, kissed

Mossy on the forehead, made him sit down on her seat, and stood before him like a servant. Mossy could not bear this, and rose at once. But the lady begged him, with tears in her beautiful eyes, to sit, and let her wait on him.

"But you are a great, splendid, beautiful lady," said Mossy.

"Yes, I am. But I work all day long—that is my pleasure; and you will have to leave me so soon!"

"How do you know that, if you please, madam?" asked Mossy.

"Because you have got the golden key."

"But I don't know what it is for. I can't find the key-hole. Will you tell me what to do?"

"You must look for the key-hole. That is your work. I cannot help you. I can only tell you that if you look for it you will find it."

"What kind of a box will it open? What is there inside?"

"I do not know. I dream about it, but I know nothing."

"Must I go at once?"

"You may stop here to-night, and have some of my supper. But you must go in the morning. All I can do for you is to give you clothes. Here is a girl called Tangle, whom you must take with you."

"That *will* be nice," said Mossy.

"No, no!" said Tangle. "I don't want to leave you, please, grandmother."

"You must go with him, Tangle. I am sorry to lose you, but it will be the best thing for you. Even the fishes, you see, have to go into the pot, and then out into the dark. If you fall in with the Old Man of the Sea, mind you ask him whether he has not got some more fishes ready for me. My tank is getting thin."

So saying, she took the fish from the pot, and put the lid on as before. They sat down and ate the fish and then the winged creature rose from the pot, circled the roof, and settled on the lady's lap. She talked to it, carried it to the door, and threw it out into the dark. They heard the flap of its wings die away in the distance.

The lady then showed Mossy into just such another chamber as that of Tangle; and in the morning he found a suit of clothes laid beside him. He looked very handsome in them. But the wearer of Grandmother's clothes never thinks about how he or she looks, but thinks always how handsome other people are.

Tangle was very unwilling to go.

"Why should I leave you? I don't know the young man," she said to the lady.

"I am never allowed to keep my children long. You need not go with him except you please, but you must go some day; and I should like you to go with him, for he has found the golden key. No girl need be afraid to go with a youth that has the golden key. You will take care of her, Mossy, will you not?"

"That I will," said Mossy.

And Tangle cast a glance at him, and thought she should like to go with him.

"And," said the lady, "if you should lose each other as you go through the—the—I never can remember the name of that country,—do not be afraid, but go on and on."

She kissed Tangle on the mouth and Mossy on the forehead, led them to the door, and waved her hand eastward. Mossy and Tangle took each other's hand and walked away into the depth of the forest. In his right hand Mossy held the golden key.

They wandered thus a long way, with endless amusement from the talk of the animals. They soon learned enough of their language to ask them necessary questions. The squirrels were always friendly, and gave them nuts out of their own hoards; but the bees were selfish and rude, justifying themselves on the ground that Tangle and Mossy were not subjects of their queen, and charity must begin at home, though indeed they had not one drone in their poorhouse at the time. Even the blinking moles would fetch them an earth-nut or a truffle now and then, talking as if their mouths, as well as their eyes and ears, were full of cotton wool, or their own velvety fur. By the time they got out of the forest they were very fond of each other, and Tangle was not in the least sorry that her grandmother had sent her away with Mossy.

At length the trees grew smaller, and stood farther apart, and the ground began to rise, and it got more and more steep, till the trees were all left behind, and the two were climbing a narrow path with rocks on each side. Suddenly they came upon a rude doorway, by which they entered a narrow gallery cut in the rock. It grew darker and darker, till it was pitch-dark, and they had to feel their way. At length the light began to return, and at last they came out upon a narrow path on the face of a lofty precipice. This path went winding down the rock to a wide plain, circular in shape, and surrounded on all sides by mountains. Those opposite to them were a great way off, and towered to an awful height, shooting up sharp, blue, ice-enamelled pinnacles. An utter silence reigned where they stood. Not even the sound of water reached them.

Looking down, they could not tell whether the valley below was a grassy plain or a great still lake. They had never seen any space look like it. The way to it was difficult and dangerous, but down the narrow path they went, and reached the bottom in safety. They found it composed of smooth, light-coloured sandstone, undulating in parts, but mostly level. It was no wonder to them now that they had not been able to tell what it was, for this surface was everywhere crowded with shadows. It was a sea of shadows. The mass was chiefly made up of the shadows of leaves innumerable, of all lovely and imaginative forms, waving to and fro, floating and quivering in the breath of a breeze whose motion was unfelt, whose sound was unheard. No forests clothed the mountain-sides, no trees were anywhere to be seen, and yet the shadows of the leaves, branches, and stems of all various trees covered the valley as far as their eyes could reach.

They soon spied the shadows of flowers mingled with those of the leaves, and now and then the shadow of a bird with open beak, and throat distended with song. At times would appear the forms of strange, graceful creatures, running up and down the shadow-boles and along the branches, to disappear in the wind-tossed foliage. As they walked they waded knee-deep in the lovely lake. For the shadows were not merely lying on the surface of the ground, but heaped up above it like substantial forms of darkness, as if they had been cast upon a thousand different planes of air. Tangle and Mossy often lifted their heads and gazed upwards to descry whence the shadows came; but they could see nothing more than a bright mist spread above them, higher than the tops of the mountains, which stood clear against it. No forests, no leaves, no birds were visible.

After a while, they reached more open spaces, where the shadows were thinner; and came even to portions over which shadows only flitted, leaving them clear for such as might follow. Now a wonderful form, half bird-like, half human, would float across on outspread sailing pinions. Anon an exquisite shadow group of gambolling children would be followed by the loveliest female form, and that again by the grand stride of a Titanic shape, each disappearing in the surrounding press of shadowy foliage. Sometimes a profile of unspeakable beauty or grandeur would appear for a moment and vanish. Sometimes they seemed lovers that passed linked arm in arm, sometimes father and son, sometimes brothers in loving contest, sometimes sisters entwined in gracefullest community of complex form. Sometimes wild horses would tear across, free, or bestrode by noble shadows of ruling men. But some of the things which pleased them most they never knew how to describe.

About the middle of the plain they sat down to rest in the heart of a heap of shadows. After sitting for a while, each, looking up, saw the other in tears: they were each longing after the country whence the shadows fell.

"We *must* find the country from which the shadows come," said Mossy.

"We must, dear Mossy," responded Tangle. "What if your golden key should be the key to *it?*"

"Ah! that would be grand," returned Mossy.—"But we must rest here for a little, and then we shall be able to cross the plain before night."

So he lay down on the ground, and about him on every side, and over his head, was the constant play of the wonderful shadows. He could look through them, and see the one behind the other, till they mixed in a mass of darkness. Tangle, too, lay admiring, and wondering, and longing after the country whence the shadows came. When they were rested they rose and pursued their journey.

How long they were in crossing this plain I cannot tell; but before night Mossy's hair was streaked with gray, and Tangle had got wrinkles on her forehead.

As evening drew on, the shadows fell deeper and rose higher. At length they reached a place where they rose above their heads, and made all dark around them. Then they took hold of each other's hand, and walked on in silence and in some dismay. They felt the gathering darkness, and something strangely solemn besides, and the beauty of the shadows ceased to delight them. All at once Tangle found that she had not a hold of Mossy's hand, though when she lost it she could not tell.

"Mossy, Mossy!" she cried aloud in terror.

But no Mossy replied.

A moment after, the shadows sank to her feet, and down under her feet, and the mountains rose before her. She turned towards the gloomy region she had left, and called once more upon Mossy. There the gloom lay tossing and heaving, a dark, stormy, foaming sea of shadows, but no Mossy rose out of it, or came climbing up the hill on which she stood. She threw herself down and wept in despair.

Suddenly she remembered that the beautiful lady had told them, if they lost each other in a country of which she could not remember the name, they were not to be afraid, but to go straight on.

"And besides," she said to herself, "Mossy has the golden key, and so no harm will come to him, I do believe."

She rose from the ground, and went on.

Before long she arrived at a precipice, in the face of which a stair was cut. When she had ascended halfway, the stair ceased, and the path led straight into the mountain. She was afraid to enter, and turning again towards the stair, grew giddy at sight of the depth beneath her, and was forced to throw herself down in the mouth of the cave.

When she opened her eyes, she saw a beautiful little creature with wings standing beside her, waiting.

"I know you," said Tangle. "You are my fish."

"Yes. But I am a fish no longer. I am an aëranth now."

"What is that?" asked Tangle.

"What you see I am," answered the shape. "And I am come to lead you through the mountain."

"Oh! thank you, dear fish—aëranth, I mean," returned Tangle, rising.

Thereupon the aëranth took to his wings, and flew on through the long, narrow passage, reminding Tangle very much of the way he had swum on before when he was a fish. And the moment his white wings moved, they began to throw off a continuous shower of sparks of all colours, which lighted up the passage before them.—All at once he vanished, and Tangle heard a low, sweet sound, quite different from the rush and crackle of his wings. Before her was an open arch, and through it came light, mixed with the sound of sea-waves.

She hurried out, and fell, tired and happy, upon the yellow sand of the shore. There she lay, half asleep with weariness and rest, listening to the low plash and retreat of the tiny waves, which seemed ever enticing the land to leave off being land, and become sea. And as she lay, her eyes were fixed upon the foot of a great rainbow standing far away against the sky on the other side of the sea. At length she fell fast asleep.

When she awoke, she saw an old man with long white hair down to his shoulders, leaning upon a stick covered with green buds, and so bending over her.

"What do you want here, beautiful woman?" he said.

"Am I beautiful? I am so glad!" answered Tangle, rising. "My grandmother is beautiful."

"Yes. But what do you want?" he repeated, kindly.

"I think I want you. Are not you the Old Man of the Sea?"

"I am."

"Then grandmother says, have you any more fishes ready for her?"

"We will go and see, my dear," answered the Old Man, speaking yet more kindly than before. "And I can do something for you, can I not?"

"Yes—show me the way up to the country from which the shadows fall," said Tangle.

For there she hoped to find Mossy again.

"Ah! indeed, that would be worth doing," said the Old Man. "But I cannot, for I do not know the way myself.

But I will send you to the Old Man of the Earth. Perhaps he can tell you. He is much older than I am."

Leaning on his staff, he conducted her along the shore to a steep rock, that looked like a petrified ship turned upside down. The door of it was the rudder of a great vessel, ages ago at the bottom of the sea. Immediately within the door was a stair in the rock, down which the Old Man went, and Tangle followed. At the bottom the Old Man had his house, and there he lived.

As soon as she entered it, Tangle heard a strange noise, unlike anything she had ever heard before. She soon found that it was the fishes talking. She tried to understand what they said; but their speech was so old-fashioned, and rude, and undefined, that she could not make much of it.

"I will go and see about those fishes for my daughter," said the Old Man of the Sea.

And moving a slide in the wall of his house, he first looked out, and then tapped upon a thick piece of crystal that filled the round opening. Tangle came up behind him, and peeping through the window into the heart of the great deep green ocean, saw the most curious creatures, some very ugly, all very odd, and with especially queer mouths, swimming about everywhere, above and below, but all coming towards the window in answer to the tap of the Old Man of the Sea. Only a few could get their mouths against the glass; but those who were floating miles away yet turned their heads towards it. The Old Man looked through the whole flock carefully for some minutes, and then turning to Tangle, said,—

"I am sorry I have not got one ready yet. I want more time than she does. But I will send some as soon as I can."

He then shut the slide.

Presently a great noise arose in the sea. The Old Man

opened the slide again, and tapped on the glass, where-upon the fishes were all as still as sleep.

"They were only talking about you," he said. "And they do speak such nonsense!—To-morrow," he contin-ued, "I must show you the way to the Old Man of the Earth. He lives a long way from here."

"Do let me go at once," said Tangle.

"No. That is not possible. You must come this way first."

He led her to a hole in the wall, which she had not observed before. It was covered with the green leaves and white blossoms of a creeping plant.

"Only white-blossoming plants can grow under the sea," said the Old Man. "In there you will find a bath, in which you must lie till I call you."

Tangle went in, and found a smaller room or cave, in the further corner of which was a great basin hollowed out of a rock, and half-full of the clearest sea-water. Little streams were constantly running into it from cracks in the wall of the cavern. It was polished quite smooth in-side, and had a carpet of yellow sand in the bottom of it. Large green leaves and white flowers of various plants crowded up over it, draping and covering it almost en-tirely.

No sooner was she undressed and lying in the bath, than she began to feel as if the water were sinking into her, and she were receiving all the good of sleep without undergoing its forgetfulness. She felt the good coming all the time. And she grew happier and more hopeful than she had been since she lost Mossy. But she could not help thinking how very sad it was for a poor old man to live there all alone, and have to take care of a whole seaful of stupid and riotous fishes.

After about an hour, as she thought, she heard his voice calling her, and rose out of the bath. All the fatigue and aching of her long journey had vanished. She was as whole, and strong, and well as if she had slept for seven days.

Returning to the opening that led into the other part of the house, she started back with amazement, for through it she saw the form of a grand man, with a majestic and beautiful face, waiting for her.

"Come," he said; "I see you are ready."

She entered with reverence.

"Where is the Old Man of the Sea?" she asked, humbly.

"There is no one here but me," he answered, smiling. "Some people call me the Old Man of the Sea. Others have another name for me, and are terribly frightened when they meet me taking a walk by the shore. Therefore I avoid being seen by them, for they are so afraid, that they never see what I really am. You see me now.—But I must show you the way to the Old Man of the Earth."

He led her into the cave where the bath was, and there she saw, in the opposite corner, a second opening in the rock.

"Go down that stair, and it will bring you to him," said the Old Man of the Sea.

With humble thanks Tangle took her leave. She went down the winding-stair, till she began to fear there was no end to it. Still down and down it went, rough and broken, with springs of water bursting out of the rocks and running down the steps beside her. It was quite dark about her, and yet she could see. For after being in that bath, people's eyes always give out a light they can see by. There were no creeping things in the way. All was safe and pleasant, though so dark and damp and deep.

At last there was not one step more, and she found herself in a glimmering cave. On a stone in the middle of it sat a figure with its back towards her—the figure of an old man bent double with age. From behind she could see his white beard spread out on the rocky floor in front of him. He did not move as she entered, so she passed round that she might stand before him and speak to him. The moment she looked in his face, she saw that he was a youth of marvellous beauty. He sat entranced with the delight of what he beheld in a mirror of something like silver, which lay on the floor at his feet, and which from behind she had taken for his white beard. He sat on, heedless of her presence, pale with the joy of his vision. She stood and watched him. At length, all trembling, she spoke. But her voice made no sound. Yet the youth lifted up his head. He showed no surprise, however, at seeing her—only smiled a welcome.

"Are you the Old Man of the Earth?" Tangle had said.

And the youth answered, and Tangle heard him, though not with her ears:—

"I am. What can I do for you?"

"Tell me the way to the country whence the shadows fall."

"Ah! that I do not know. I only dream about it myself. I see its shadows sometimes in my mirror: the way to it I do not know. But I think the Old Man of the Fire must know. He is much older than I am. He is the oldest man of all."

"Where does he live?"

"I will show you the way to his place. I never saw him myself."

So saying, the young man rose, and then stood a while gazing at Tangle.

"I wish I could see that country too," he said. "But I must mind my work."

He led her to the side of the cave, and told her to lay her ear against the wall.

"What do you hear?" he asked.

152

"I hear," answered Tangle, "the sound of a great water running inside the rock."

"That river runs down to the dwelling of the oldest man of all—the Old Man of the Fire. I wish I could go to see him. But I must mind my work. That river is the only way to him."

Then the Old Man of the Earth stooped over the floor of the cave, raised a huge stone from it, and left it leaning. It disclosed a great hole that went plumb-down.

"That is the way," he said.

"But there are no stairs."

"You must throw yourself in. There is no other way."

She turned and looked him full in the face—stood so for a whole minute, as she thought: it was a whole year—then threw herself headlong into the hole.

When she came to herself, she found herself gliding down fast and deep. Her head was under water, but that did not signify, for, when she thought about it she could not remember that she had breathed once since her bath in the cave of the Old Man of the Sea. When she lifted up her head a sudden and fierce heat struck her, and she dropped it again instantly, and went sweeping on.

Gradually the stream grew shallower. At length she could hardly keep her head under. Then the water could carry her no farther. She rose from the channel, and went step for step down the burning descent. The water ceased altogether. The heat was terrible. She felt scorched to the bone, but it did not touch her strength. It grew hotter and hotter. She said, "I can bear it no longer." Yet she went on.

At the long last, the stair ended at a rude archway in an all but glowing rock. Through this archway Tangle fell exhausted into a cool mossy cave. The floor and walls were covered with moss—green, soft, and damp. A little stream spouted from a rent in the rock and fell into a basin of moss. She plunged her face into it and drank. Then she lifted her head and looked around. Then she rose and looked again. She saw no one in the cave. But the moment she stood upright she had a marvellous sense that she was in the secret of the earth and all its ways. Everything she had seen, or learned from books; all that her grandmother had said or sung to her; all the talk of the beasts, birds, and fishes; all that had happened to her on her journey with Mossy, and since then in the heart of the earth with the Old Man and the Older Man—all was plain: she understood it all, and saw that everything meant the same thing, though she could not have put it into words again.

The next moment she descried, in a corner of the cave, a little naked child, sitting on the moss. He was playing with balls of various colours and sizes, which he disposed in strange figures upon the floor beside him. And now Tangle felt that there was something in her knowledge which was not in her understanding. For she knew there must be an infinite meaning in the change and sequence and individual forms of the figures into which the child arranged the balls, as well as in the varied harmonies of their colours, but what it all meant she could not tell.

He went on busily, tirelessly, playing his solitary game, without looking up, or seeming to know that there was a stranger in his deep-withdrawn cell. Diligently as a lace-maker shifts her bobbins, he shifted and arranged his balls. Flashes of meaning would now pass from them to Tangle, and now again all would be not merely obscure, but utterly dark. She stood looking for a long time, for there was fascination in the sight; and the longer she looked the more an indescribable vague intelligence went on rousing itself in her mind. For seven years she had stood there watching the naked Child with his coloured balls, and it seemed to her like seven hours, when all at once the shape the balls took, she knew not why, reminded her of the Valley of Shadows, and she spoke:—

"Where is the Old Man of the Fire?" she said.

"Here I am," answered the Child, rising and leaving his balls on the moss. "What can I do for you?"

There was such an awfulness of absolute repose on the face of the Child that Tangle stood dumb before him. He had no smile, but the love in his large gray eyes was deep as the centre. And with the repose there lay on his face a shimmer as of moonlight, which seemed as if any moment it might break into such a ravishing smile as would cause the beholder to weep himself to death. But the smile never came, and the moonlight lay there unbroken. For the heart of the child was too deep for any smile to reach from it to his face.

"Are you the oldest man of all?" Tangle at length, although filled with awe, ventured to ask.

"Yes, I am. I am very, very old. I am able to help you, I know. I can help everybody."

And the Child drew near and looked up in her face so that she burst into tears.

"Can you tell me the way to the country the shadows fall from?" she sobbed.

"Yes. I know the way quite well. I go there myself sometimes. But you could not go my way; you are not old enough. I will show you how you can go."

"Do not send me out into the great heat again," prayed Tangle.

"I will not," answered the Child.

And he reached up, and put his little cool hand on her heart.

"Now," he said, "you can go. The fire will not burn you. Come."

He led her from the cave, and following him through another archway, she found herself in a vast desert of sand and rock. The sky of it was of rock, lowering over them like solid thunder-clouds; and the whole place was so hot that she saw, in bright rivulets, the yellow gold and white silver and red copper trickling molten from the rocks. But the heat never came near her.

When they had gone some distance, the Child turned up a great stone, and took something like an egg from under it. He next drew a long curved line in the sand with his finger, and laid the egg in it. He then spoke something Tangle could not understand. The egg broke, a small snake came out, and, lying in the line in the sand, grew and grew till he filled it. The moment he was thus full-grown, he began to glide away, undulating like a sea-wave.

"Follow that serpent," said the Child. "He will lead you the right way."

Tangle followed the serpent. But she could not go far without looking back at the marvellous Child. He stood alone in the midst of the glowing desert, beside a fountain of red flame that had burst forth at his feet, his naked whiteness glimmering a pale rosy red in the torrid fire. There he stood, looking after her, till, from the lengthening distance, she could see him no more. The serpent went straight on, turning neither to the right nor left.

Meantime Mossy had got out of the lake of shadows, and, following his mournful, lonely way, had reached the sea-shore. It was a dark, stormy evening. The sun had set. The wind was blowing from the sea. The waves had surrounded the rock within which lay the Old Man's house. A deep water rolled between it and the shore, upon which a majestic figure was walking alone.

Mossy went up to him and said,—

"Will you tell me where to find the Old Man of the Sea?"

"I am the Old Man of the Sea," the figure answered.

"I see a strong kingly man of middle age," returned Mossy.

Then the Old Man looked at him more intently, and said,—

"Your sight, young man, is better than that of most who take this way. The night is stormy: come to my house and tell me what I can do for you."

Mossy followed him. The waves flew from before the footsteps of the Old Man of the Sea, and Mossy followed upon dry sand.

When they had reached the cave, they sat down and gazed at each other.

Now Mossy was an old man by this time. He looked much older than the Old Man of the Sea, and his feet were very weary.

After looking at him for a moment, the Old Man took him by the hand and led him into his inner cave. There he helped him to undress, and laid him in the bath. And he saw that one of his hands Mossy did not open.

"What have you in that hand?" he asked.

Mossy opened his hand, and there lay the golden key.

"Ah!" said the Old Man, "that accounts for your knowing me. And I know the way you have to go."

"I want to find the country whence the shadows fall," said Mossy.

"I dare say you do. So do I. But meantime, one thing is certain.—What is that key for, do you think?"

"For a keyhole somewhere. But I don't know why I keep it. I never could find the keyhole. And I have lived a good while, I believe," said Mossy, sadly. "I'm not sure that I'm not old. I know my feet ache."

"Do they?" said the Old Man, as if he really meant to ask the question; and Mossy, who was still lying in the bath, watched his feet for a moment before he replied.

"No, they do not," he answered. "Perhaps I am not old either."

"Get up and look at yourself in the water."

He rose and looked at himself in the water, and there was not a gray hair on his head or a wrinkle on his skin.

"You have tasted of death now," said the Old Man. "Is it good?"

"It is good," said Mossy. "It is better than life."

"No," said the Old Man: "it is only more life.—Your feet will make no holes in the water now."

"What do you mean?"

"I will show you that presently."

They turned to the outer cave, and sat and talked together for a long time. At length the Old Man of the Sea arose and said to Mossy,—

"Follow me."

He led him up the stair again, and opened another door. They stood on the level of the raging sea, looking towards the east. Across the waste of waters, against the bosom of a fierce black cloud, stood the foot of a rainbow, glowing in the dark.

"This indeed is my way," said Mossy, as soon as he saw the rainbow, and stepped out upon the sea. His feet made no holes in the water. He fought the wind, and clomb the waves, and went on towards the rainbow.

The storm died away. A lovely day and a lovelier night followed. A cool wind blew over the wide plain of the quiet ocean. And still Mossy journeyed eastward. But the rainbow had vanished with the storm.

Day after day he held on, and he thought he had no guide. He did not see how a shining fish under the waters directed his steps. He crossed the sea, and came to a great precipice of rock, up which he could discover but one path. Nor did this lead him farther than half-way up the rock, where it ended on a platform. Here he stood and pondered.—It could not be that the way stopped here, else what was the path for? It was a rough path, not very plain, yet certainly a path.—He examined the face of the rock. It was smooth as glass. But as his eyes kept roving hopelessly over it, something glittered, and he caught sight of a row of small sapphires. They bordered a little hole in the rock.

"The keyhole!" he cried.

He tried the key. It fitted. It turned. A great clang and clash, as of iron bolts on huge brazen caldrons echoed thunderously within. He drew out the key. The rock in front of him began to fall. He retreated from it as far as the breadth of the platform would allow. A great slab fell at his feet. In front was still the solid rock, with this one slab fallen forward out of it.

But the moment he stepped upon it, a second fell, just short of the edge of the first, making the next step of a stair, which thus kept dropping itself before him as he ascended into the heart of the precipice. It led him into a hall fit for such an approach—irregular and rude in formation, but floor, sides, pillars, and vaulted roof, all one mass of shining stones of every colour that light can show. In the centre stood seven columns, ranged from red to violet. And on the pedestal of one of them sat a woman, motionless, with her face bowed upon her knees. Seven years had she sat there waiting. She lifted her head as Mossy drew near. It was Tangle. Her hair had grown to her feet, and was rippled like the windless sea on broad sands. Her face was beautiful, like her grandmother's, and as still and peaceful as that of the Old Man of the Fire. Her form was tall and noble. Yet Mossy knew her at once.

"How beautiful you are, Tangle!" he said, in delight and astonishment.

"Am I?" she returned. "Oh, I have waited for you so long! But you, you are like the Old Man of the Sea. No. You are like the Old Man of the Earth. No, no. You are

like the oldest man of all. You are like them all. And yet
you are my own old Mossy! How did you come here?
What did you do after I lost you? Did you find the keyhole? Have you got the key still?"

She had a hundred questions to ask him, and he a hundred more to ask her. They told each other all their adventures, and were as happy as man and woman could
be. For they were younger and better, and stronger and
wiser, than they had ever been before.

It began to grow dark. And they wanted more than
ever to reach the country whence the shadows fall. So
they looked about them for a way out of the cave. The
door by which Mossy entered had closed again, and
there was half a mile of rock between them and the sea.
Neither could Tangle find the opening in the floor by
which the serpent had led her thither. They searched till
it grew so dark that they could see nothing, and gave it
up.

After a while, however, the cave began to glimmer
again. The light came from the moon, but it did not look
like moonlight, for it gleamed through those seven pillars in the middle, and filled the place with all colours.
And now Mossy saw that there was a pillar beside the
red one, which he had not observed before. And it was of
the same new colour that he had seen in the rainbow
when he saw it first in the fairy forest. And on it he saw a
sparkle of blue. It was the sapphires round the keyhole.

He took the key. It turned in the lock to the sounds of
Æolian music. A door opened upon slow hinges, and disclosed a winding stair within. The key vanished from his
fingers. Tangle went up. Mossy followed. The door
closed behind them. They climbed out of the earth; and,
still climbing, rose above it. They were in the rainbow.
Far abroad, over ocean and land, they could see through
its transparent walls the earth beneath their feet. Stairs

beside stairs wound up together, and beautiful beings of all ages climbed along with them.

They knew that they were going up to the country whence the shadows fell.

And by this time I think they must have got there.

MacDonald's sermons appear primarily in three series titled Unspoken Sermons. The first of these series was published in 1867. "The Cry, 'Eloi, Eloi'" is taken from this first volume and deals with Christ's sufferings. MacDonald finds that although Christ endured the most intense suffering and most severe trial that men can face when He was on the cross, His will was triumphant. His cry on the cross was a cry of desolation, but it was also a cry of faith. In the same way, even when we cannot feel God's presence or feel like doing good, we must nevertheless continue to hold fast to God.

Though the law cannot fulfill love, love can fulfill the law is a theme MacDonald uses in "Love Thy Neighbour," which is also from the first volume of sermons. MacDonald sets out to answer the question of how we may love our neighbors and arrives at the conclusion that we must begin by obedience. Once a man has united himself with God by obedient action, the truth of love is made known to him. Human society is built upon two loves: love for God and love for man. It is only in loving our neighbor that we can truly show love for God.

"The God of the Living" starts with Christ's answer to the Sadducees concerning the resurrection of the dead, a theme MacDonald was fond of discussing. MacDonald's sacramental theology is revealed here when he discusses the nature of our present bodies and states that they are "the means of revelation to us, the camera in which God's eternal shows are set forth." Our resurrection bodies will fulfill the same function as our present ones, only more gloriously.

CHAPTER FIVE

The Cry, "Eloi, Eloi"

"My God, my God, why hast thou forsaken me?" (Matt. 27:46).

I do not know that I should dare to approach this of all utterances into which human breath has ever been moulded, most awful in import, did I not feel that, containing both germ and blossom of the final devotion, it contains therefore the deepest practical lesson the human heart has to learn. The Lord, the Revealer, hides nothing that can be revealed, and will not warn away the foot that treads in naked humility even upon the ground of that terrible conflict between him and evil, when the smoke of the battle, that was fought not only with garments rolled in blood but with burning and fuel of fire, rose up between him and his Father, and, for the one terrible moment ere he broke the bonds of life, and walked weary and triumphant into his arms, hid God from the eyes of his Son. He will give us even to meditate the one thought that slew him at last, when he could bear no more, and fled to the Father to know that he loved him, and was well pleased with him.

For Satan had come at length yet again, to urge him

with his last temptation; to tell him that although he had done his part, God had forgotten his; that although he had lived by the word of his mouth, that mouth had no word more to speak to him; that although he had refused to tempt him, God had left him to be tempted more than he could bear; that although he had worshiped none other, for that worship God did not care. The Lord hides not his sacred sufferings, for truth is light, and would be light in the minds of men. The Holy Child, the Son of the Father, has nothing to conceal, but all the Godhead to reveal. Let us then put off our shoes, and draw near, and bow the head, and kiss those feet that bear forever the scars of our victory. In those feet we clasp the safety of our suffering, our sinning brotherhood.

Christ's Perfect Will

It is with the holiest fear that we should approach the terrible fact of the sufferings of our Lord. Let no one think that those were less because he was more. The more delicate the nature, the more alive to all that is lovely and true, lawful and right, the more does it feel the antagonism of pain, the inroad of death upon life; the more dreadful is that breach of the harmony of things whose sound is torture. He felt more than man could feel, because he had a larger feeling. He was even therefore worn out sooner than another man would have been.

These sufferings were awful indeed when they began to invade the region about the will; when the struggle to keep consciously trusting in God began to sink in darkness; when the will of The Man put forth its last determined effort in that cry after the vanishing vision of the Father: *My God, my God, why hast thou forsaken me?* Never had it been so with him before. Never before had he been unable to see God beside him. Yet never was God nearer him than now. For never was Jesus more divine. He could not see, could not feel him near; and yet it is "*My* God" that he cries.

Thus the will of Jesus, in the very moment when his faith seems about to yield, is finally triumphant. It has no *feeling* now to support it, no beatific vision to absorb it. It stands naked in his soul and tortured, as he stood naked and scourged before Pilate. Pure and simple and surrounded by fire, it declares for God. The sacrifice ascends in the cry, *My God*. The cry comes not out of happiness, out of peace, out of hope. Not even out of suffering comes that cry. It was a cry *in* desolation, but it came out of faith. It is the last voice of truth, speaking when it can but cry. The divine horror of that moment is unfathomable by human soul. It was blackness of darkness. And yet he would believe. Yet he would hold fast. God was his God yet. *My God*—and in the cry came forth the victory, and all was over soon. Of the peace that followed that cry, the peace of a perfect soul, large as the universe, pure as light, ardent as life, victorious for God and his brethren, he himself alone can ever know the breadth and length, and depth and height.

Without this last trial of all, the temptations of our Master had not been so full as the human cup could hold; there would have been one region through which we had to pass wherein we might call aloud upon our Captain-Brother, and there would be no voice or hearing: he had avoided the fatal spot! The temptations of the desert came to the young, strong man with his road before him, and the presence of his God around him; nay, gathered their very force from the exuberance of his conscious faith. "Dare and do, for God is with thee," said the devil. "I know it, and therefore I will wait," returned the king of his brothers.

And now, after three years of divine action, when his course is run, when the old age of finished work is come, when the whole frame is tortured until the regnant brain falls whirling down the blue gulf of fainting, and the giving up of the ghost is at hand, when the friends have forsaken him and fled, comes the voice of the enemy again at his ear: "Despair and die, for God is not with thee. All is in vain. Death, not life, is thy refuge. Make haste to Hades, where thy torture will be over. Thou hast deceived thyself. He never was with thee. He was the God of Abraham. Abraham is dead. Whom makest thou thyself?"

"My God, my God, why hast thou forsaken me?" the Master cries. For God was his God still, although he had forsaken him—forsaken *his vision* that his faith might glow out triumphant; forsaken *himself?* no; come nearer to him than ever: come nearer, even as—but with a yet deeper, more awful pregnancy of import—even as the Lord himself withdrew from the bodily eyes of his friends, that he might dwell in their profoundest being.

I do not think it was our Lord's deepest trial when in the garden he prayed that the cup might pass from him, and prayed yet again that the will of the Father might be done. For that will was then present with him. He was living and acting in that will. But now the foreseen horror has come. He is drinking the dread cup, and The Will has vanished from his eyes. Were that Will visible in his suffering, his will could bow with tearful gladness under the shelter of its grandeur. But now his will is left alone to drink the cup of The Will in torture. In the sickness of this agony, the will of Jesus arises perfect at last; and of itself, unsupported now, declares—a naked consciousness of misery hung in the waste darkness of the universe—declares for God, in defiance of pain, of death, of apathy, of self, of negation, of the blackness within and around it; calls aloud upon the vanished God.

This is the Faith of the Son of God. God withdrew, as it were, that the perfect will of the Son might arise and go forth to find the will of the Father.

Is it possible that even then he thought of the lost sheep who could not believe that God was their Father; and for them, too, in all their loss and blindness and un-love, cried, saying the word they might say, knowing for them that *God* means *Father* and more, and knowing now, as he had never known till now, what a fearful thing it is to be without God and without hope? I dare not answer the question I put.

Creeping about in the Valleys

But wherein or what can this Alpine apex of faith have to do with the creatures who call themselves Christians, creeping about in the valleys, hardly knowing that there are mountains above them, save that they take offence at, and stumble over, the pebbles washed across their path by the glacier streams? I will tell you. We are and remain such creeping Christians, because we look at ourselves and not at Christ; because we gaze at the marks of our own soiled feet, and the trail of our own defiled garments, instead of up at the snows of purity, whither the soul of Christ clomb.

Each, putting his foot in the footprint of the Master, and so defacing it, turns to examine how far his neighbor's footprint corresponds with that which he still calls the Master's, although it is but his own. Or, having committed a petty fault, I mean a fault such as only a petty creature could commit, we mourn over the defilement to ourselves, and the shame of it before our friends, children, or servants, instead of hastening to make the due confession and amends to our fellow, and then, forgetting our paltry self, with its well-earned disgrace, lift up our eyes to the glory which alone will quicken the true man in us, and kill the peddling creature we so wrongly call our *self*. The true self is that which can look Jesus in the face, and say, *My Lord*.

When the inward sun is shining, and the wind of

thought, blowing where it lists amid the flowers and leaves of fancy and imagination, rouses glad forms and feelings, it is easy to look upwards, and say, *My God*. It is easy when the frosts of external failure have braced the mental nerves to healthy endurance and fresh effort after labor, it is easy then to turn to God and trust in him, in whom all honest exertion gives an ability as well as a right to trust. It is easy in pain, so long as it does not pass certain undefinable bounds, to hope in God for deliverance, or pray for strength to endure.

But what is to be done when all feeling is gone? when a man does not know whether he believes or not, whether he loves or not? when art, poetry, religion are nothing to him, so swallowed up is he in pain, or mental depression, or disappointment, or temptation, or he knows not what? It seems to him then that God does not care for him, and certainly he does not care for God. If he is still humble, he thinks that he is so bad that God cannot care for him. And he then believes for the time that God loves us only because and when and while we love him; instead of believing that God loves us always because he is our God, and that we live only by his love. Or he does not believe in a God at all, which is better.

So long as we have nothing to say to God, nothing to do with him, save in the sunshine of the mind when we feel him near us, we are poor creatures, willed upon, not willing; reeds, flowering reeds, it may be, and pleasant to behold, but only reeds blown about of the wind; not bad, but poor creatures.

And how, in such a condition, do we generally act? Do we not sit mourning over the loss of our feelings? or worse, make frantic efforts to rouse them? or ten times worse, relapse into a state of temporary atheism, and yield to the pressing temptation? or, being heartless, consent to remain careless, conscious of evil thoughts and low feelings alone, but too lazy, too content to rouse ourselves against them? We know we must get rid of them some day, but meantime—never mind; we do not *feel* them bad, we do not feel anything else good; we are asleep and we know it, and we cannot be troubled to wake. No impulse comes to arouse us, and so we remain as we are.

God does not, by the instant gift of his Spirit, make us always feel right, desire good, love purity, aspire after him and his will. Therefore either he will not, or he cannot. If he will not, it must be because it would not be well to do so. If he cannot, then he would not if he could; else a better condition than God is conceivable to the mind of God—a condition in which he could save the creatures whom he has made, better than he can save them. The truth is this: He wants to make us in his own image, *choosing* the good, *refusing* the evil. How should he effect this if he were *always* moving us from within, as he does at divine intervals, towards the beauty of holiness? God gives us room *to be;* does not oppress us with his will; "stands away from us," that we may act from ourselves, that we may exercise the pure will for good.

Do not, therefore, imagine me to mean that we can do anything of ourselves without God. If we choose the right at last, it is all God's doing, and only the more his that it is ours, only in a far more marvelous way his than if he had kept us filled with all holy impulses precluding the need of choice. For up to this very point, for this very point, he has been educating us, leading us, pushing us, driving us, enticing us, that we may choose him and his will, and so be tenfold more his children, of his own best making, in the freedom of the will found our own first in its loving sacrifice to him, for which in his grand fatherhood he has been thus working from the foundations of the earth, than we could be in the most ecstatic worship flowing from the divinest impulse, without this *willing* sacrifice.

For God made our individuality as well as, and a greater marvel than, our dependence; made our *apart-ness* from himself, that freedom should bind us divinely dearer to himself, with a new and inscrutable marvel of love; for the Godhead is still at the root, is the making root of our individuality, and the freer the man, the stronger the bond that binds him to him who made his freedom. He made our wills, and is striving to make them free; for only in the perfection of our individuality and the freedom of our wills can we be altogether his children. This is full of mystery, but can we not see enough in it to make us very glad and very peaceful?

Not in any other act than one which, in spite of impulse or of weakness, declares for the truth, for God, does the will spring into absolute freedom, into true life.

Making Our Wills One with God's

See, then, what lies within our reach every time that we are thus lapped in the folds of night. The highest condition of the human will is in sight, is attainable. I say not the highest condition of the human being; that surely lies in the beatific vision, in the sight of God. But the highest condition of the human will, as distinct, not as separated from God, is when, not seeing God, not seeming to itself to grasp him at all, it yet holds him fast. It cannot continue in this condition, for, not finding, not seeing God, the man would die; but the will thus asserting itself, the man has passed from death into life, and the vision is nigh at hand.

Then first, thus free, in thus asserting its freedom, is the individual will one with the will of God; the child is finally restored to the father; the childhood and the fatherhood meet in one; the brotherhood of the race arises from the dust; and the prayer of our Lord is answered, "I in them and thou in me, that they may be made perfect in one." Let us then arise in God-born strength every time that we feel the darkness closing, or become aware that it has closed around us, and say, "I am of the light and not of the darkness."

Troubled soul, thou art not bound to feel, but thou art bound to arise. God loves thee whether thou feelest or not. Thou canst not love when thou wilt, but thou art bound to fight the hatred in thee to the last. Try not to feel good when thou art not good, but cry to him who is good. He changes not because thou changest. Nay, he has an especial tenderness of love towards thee for that thou art in the dark, and hast no light, and his heart is glad when thou dost arise and say, "I will go to my Father." For he sees thee through all the gloom through which thou canst not see him.

Will thou his will. Say unto him: "My God, I am very dull and low and hard; but thou art wise and high and tender, and thou art my God. I am thy child. Forsake me not." Then fold the arms of thy faith, and wait in quietness until light goes up in thy darkness. Fold the arms of thy faith I say, but not of thy action: bethink thee of something that thou oughtest to do, and go and do it, if it be but the sweeping of a room, or the preparing of a meal, or a visit to a friend. Heed not thy feelings: Do thy work.

As God lives by his own will, and we live in him, so has he given to us power to will in ourselves. How much better should we not fare if, finding that we are standing with our heads bowed away from the good, finding that we have no feeble inclination to seek the source of our life, we should yet *will* upwards toward God, rousing that essence of life in us, which he has given us from his own heart, to call again upon him who is our life, who can fill the emptiest heart, rouse the deadest conscience, quicken the dullest feeling, and strengthen the feeblest will!

Then, if ever the time should come, as perhaps it must come to each of us, when all consciousness of well-being shall have vanished, when the earth shall be but a sterile promontory, and the heavens a dull and pestilent congregation of vapors, when man nor woman shall delight us more, nay, when God himself shall be but a name, and Jesus an old story, then, even then, when a death far worse than "that phantom of grisly bone" is griping at our hearts, and having slain love, hope, faith, forces existence upon us only in agony, then, even then, we shall be able to cry out with our Lord, "My God, my God, why hast thou forsaken me?" Nor shall we die then, I think, without being able to take up his last words as well, and say, *"Father, into thy hands I commend my spirit."*

CHAPTER SIX

Love Thy Neighbour

Thou shalt love thy neighbour as thyself (Matt. 23:39).

The original here quoted by our Lord is to be found in the words of God to Moses *(Lev. 19:18), "Thou shalt not avenge, nor bear any grudge against the children of thy people, but thou shalt love thy neighbour as thyself: I am the Lord."* Our Lord never thought of being original. The older the saying the better, if it utters the truth he wants to utter. In him it becomes fact: The *Word* was made *flesh*. And so, in the wondrous meeting of extremes, the words he spoke were no more words, but spirit and life.

Love and the Law

The same words are twice quoted by St. Paul, and once by St. James, always in a similar mode: Love they represent as the fulfilling of the law.

Is the converse true then? Is the fulfilling of the law love? The apostle Paul says: "Love worketh no ill to his neighbour, therefore love is the fulfilling of the law."

Does it follow that *working no ill* is love? Love will fulfil the law: will the law fulfil love? No, verily. If a man keeps the law, I know he is a lover of his neighbour. But he is not a lover because he keeps the law: he keeps the law because he is a lover. No heart will be content with the law for love. The law cannot fulfil love.

"But, at least, the law will be able to fulfil itself, though it reaches not to love."

I do not believe it. I am certain that it is impossible to keep the law towards one's neighbour except one loves him. The law itself is infinite, reaching to such delicacies of action, that the man who tries most will be the man most aware of defeat. We are not made for law, but for love. Love is law, because it is infinitely more than law. It is of an altogether higher region than law—is, in fact, the creator of law. Had it not been for love, not one of the *shalt-nots* of the law would have been uttered. True, once uttered, they shew themselves in the form of justice, yea, even in the inferior and worldly forms of prudence and self-preservation; but it was love that spoke them first.

Were there no love in us, what sense of justice could we have? Would not each be filled with the sense of his own wants, and be for ever tearing to himself? I do not say it is *conscious* love that breeds justice, but I do say that without love in our nature justice would never be born. For I do not call that justice which consists only in a sense of *our own* rights. True, there are poor and withered forms of love which are immeasurably below justice now; but even now they are of speechless worth, for they will grow into that which will supersede, because it will necessitate, justice.

Fulfilling the Law

Of what use then is the law? To lead us to Christ, the Truth,—to waken in our minds a sense of what our deepest nature, the presence, namely, of God *in* us, requires of us,—to let us know, in part by failure, that the purest effort of will of which we are capable cannot lift us up even to the abstaining from wrong to our neighbour. What man, for instance, who loves not his neighbour and yet wishes to keep the law, will dare be confident that never by word, look, tone, gesture, silence, will he bear false witness against that neighbour? What man can judge his neighbour aright save him whose love makes him refuse to judge him? Therefore are we told to love, and not judge. It is the sole justice of which we are capable, and that perfected will comprise all justice. Nay more, to refuse our neighbour love, is to do him the greatest wrong.

But of this afterwards. In order to fulfil the commonest law, I repeat, we must rise into a loftier region altogether, a region that is above law, because it is spirit and life and makes the law: in order to keep the law towards our neighbour, we must love our neighbour. We are not made for law, but for grace—or for faith, to use another word so much misused. We are made on too large a scale altogether to have any pure relation to mere justice, if indeed we can say there is such a thing. It is but an abstract idea which, in reality, will not be abstracted. The law comes to make us long for the needful grace,—that is, for the divine condition, in which love is all, for God is Love.

Though the fulfilling of the law is the practical form love will take, and the neglect of it is the conviction of lovelessness; though it is the mode in which a man's *will* must begin at once to be love to his neighbour, yet, that our Lord meant by the love of our neighbour, not the fulfilling of the law towards him, but that condition of being which results in the fulfilling of the law and more, is sufficiently clear from his story of the good Samaritan. "Who is my neighbour?" said the lawyer. And the Lord taught him that every one to whom he could be or for whom he could do anything was his neighbour; therefore, that each of the race, as he comes within the touch of one tentacle of our nature, is our neighbour. Which of the inhibitions of the law is illustrated in the tale? Not one. The love that is more than law, and renders its breach impossible, lives in the endless story, coming out in active kindness, that is, the recognition of kin, of *kind*, of nighness, of *neighbourhood;* yea, in tenderness and loving-kindness—the Samaritan-heart akin to the Jew-heart, the Samaritan hands neighbours to the Jewish wounds.

Thou shalt love thy neighbour as thyself.

So direct and complete is this parable of our Lord, that one becomes almost ashamed of further talk about it. Suppose a man of the company had put the same question to our Lord that we have been considering had said, "But I may keep the law and yet not love my neighbour," would he not have returned: "Keep thou the law thus, not in the letter, but in the spirit, that is, in the truth of action, and thou wilt soon find, O Jew, that thou lovest thy Samaritan"? And yet, when thoughts and questions arise in our minds, he desires that we should follow them. He will not check us with a word of heavenly wisdom scornfully uttered. He knows that not even *his* words will apply to every question of the willing soul; and we know that his spirit will reply. When we want to know more, that more will be there for us. Not every man, for instance, finds his neighbour in need of help, and he would gladly hasten the slow results of opportunity by true thinking. Thus would we be ready for further teaching from that Spirit who is the Lord.

Learning to Love Thy Neighbour

"But how," says a man, who is willing to recognize the universal neighbourhead, but finds himself unable to fulfil the bare law towards the woman even whom he loves best,—"How am I then to rise into that higher region, that empyrean of love?" And, beginning straightway to try to love his neighbour, he finds that the empyrean of which he spoke is no more to be reached in itself than the law was to be reached in itself. As he cannot keep the law without first rising into the love of his neighbour, so he cannot love his neighbour without first rising higher still.

The whole system of the universe works upon this law—the driving of things upward towards the centre. The man who will love his neighbour can do so by no immediately operative exercise of the will. It is the man fulfilled of God from whom he came and by whom he is, who alone can as himself love his neighbour who came from God too and is by God too.

The mystery of individuality and consequent relation is deep as the beginnings of humanity, and the questions thence arising can be solved only by him who has, practically, at least, solved the holy necessities resulting from his origin. In God alone can man meet man. In him alone the converging lines of existence touch and cross not. When the mind of Christ, the life of the Head, courses through that atom which the man is of the slowly revivifying body, when he is alive too, then the love of the brothers is there as conscious life. From Christ through the neighbours comes the life that makes him a part of the body.

It *is* possible to love our neighbour as ourselves. Our Lord *never spoke* hyperbolically, although, indeed, that is the supposition on which many unconsciously interpret his words, in order to be able to persuade themselves that they believe them. We may see that it is possible before we attain to it; for our perceptions of truth are always in advance of our condition.

True, no man can see it perfectly until he is it; but we must see it, that we may be it. A man who knows that he does not yet love his neighbour as himself may believe in such a condition, may even see that there is no other goal of human perfection, nothing else to which the universe is speeding, propelled by the Father's will. Let him labour on, and not faint at the thought that God's day is a thousand years: millennium is likewise one day—yea, this day, for we have him, The Love, in us, working even now the far end.

Steps to Loving Thy Neighbour

But while it is true that only when a man loves God with all his heart, will he love his neighbour as himself, yet there are mingled processes in the attainment of this final result. Let us try to aid such operation of truth by looking farther. Let us suppose that the man who believes our Lord both meant what he said, and knew the truth of the matter, proceeds to endeavour obedience in this of loving his neighbour as himself. He begins to think about his neighbours generally, and he tries to feel love towards them.

He finds at once that they begin to classify themselves. With some he feels no difficulty, for he loves them already, not indeed because they *are*, but because they have, by friendly qualities, by showing themselves lovable, that is loving, already, moved his feelings as the wind moves the waters, that is without any self-generated action on his part. And he feels that this is nothing much to the point; though, of course, he would be farther from the desired end if he had none such to love, and farther still if he loved none such.

He recalls the words of our Lord, "If ye love them which love you, what reward have ye?" and his mind fixes upon—let us say—one of a second class, and he tries to love him. The man is no enemy—we have not come to that class of neighbours yet—but he is dull, uninteresting—in a negative way, he thinks, unlovable.

What is he to do with him? With all his effort, he finds the goal as far off as ever.

Naturally, in his failure, the question arises, "Is it my duty to love him who is unlovable?"

Certainly not, if he is unlovable. But that is a begging of the question.

Thereupon the man falls back on the primary foundation of things, and asks—

"How, then, is the man to be loved by me? Why should I love my neighbour as myself?"

We must not answer "Because the Lord says so." It is because the Lord says so that the man is inquiring after some help to obey. No man can love his neighbour *merely* because the Lord says so. The Lord says so because it is right and necessary and natural, and the man wants to feel it thus right and necessary and natural. Although the Lord would be pleased with any man for doing a thing because he said it, he would show his pleasure by making the man more and more dissatisfied until he knew why the Lord had said it. He would make him see that he could not in the deepest sense—in the way the Lord loves—obey any command until he saw the reasonableness of it.

Observe I do not say the man ought to put off obeying the command until he see its reasonableness: that is another thing quite, and does not lie in the scope of my present supposition. It is a beautiful thing to obey the rightful source of a command: it is a more beautiful thing to worship the radiant source of our light, and it is for the sake of obedient vision that our Lord commands us. For then our heart meets his: we see God.

Why Should I Love My Neighbour?

Let me represent in the form of a conversation what might pass in the man's mind on the opposing sides of the question.—"Why should I love my neighbour?"

181

"He is the same as I, and therefore I ought to love him."

"Why? I am I. He is he."

"He has the same thoughts, feelings, hopes, sorrows, joys, as I."

"Yes; but why should I love him for that? He must mind his, I can only do with mine."

"He has the same consciousness as I have. As things look to me, so things look to him."

"Yes; but I cannot get into his consciousness, nor he into mine. I feel myself; I do not feel him. My life flows through my veins, not through his. The world shines into my consciousness, and I am not conscious of his consciousness. I wish I could love him, but I do not see why. I am an individual; he is an individual. My self must be closer to me than he can be. Two bodies keep me apart from his self. I am isolated with myself."

Love in Action

Now, here lies the mistake at last. While the thinker supposes a duality in himself which does not exist, he falsely judges the individuality a separation. On the contrary, it is the sole possibility and very bond of love. *Otherness* is the essential ground of affection. But in spiritual things, such a unity is pre-supposed in the very contemplation of them by the spirit of man, that wherever anything does not exist that ought to be there, the space it ought to occupy, even if but a blank, assumes the appearance of a separating gulf. The negative looks a positive.

Where a man does not love, the not-loving must seem rational. For no one loves because he sees why, but because he loves. No human reason can be given for the highest necessity of divinely created existence. For reasons are always from above downwards. A man must just feel this necessity, and then questioning is over. It justifies itself. But he who has not felt has it not to argue about. He has but its phantom, which he created himself in a vain effort to understand, and which he supposes to be it.

Love cannot be argued about in its absence, for there is no reflex, no symbol of it near enough to the fact of it, to admit of just treatment by the algebra of the reason or imagination. Indeed, the very talking about it raises a mist between the mind and the vision of it. But let a man once love, and all those difficulties which appeared opposed to love, will just be so many arguments for loving.

Let a man once find another who has fallen among thieves; let him be a neighbour to him, pouring oil and wine into his wounds, and binding them up, and setting him on his own beast, and paying for him at the inn; let him do all this merely from a sense of duty; let him even, in the pride of his fancied, and the ignorance of his true calling, bate no jot of his Jewish superiority; let him condescend to the very baseness of his own lowest nature; yet such will be the virtue of obeying an eternal truth even to his poor measure, of putting in actuality what he has not even seen in theory, of doing the truth even without believing it, that even if the truth does not after the deed give the faintest glimmer as truth in the man, he will yet be ages nearer the truth than before, for he will go on his way loving that Samaritan neighbour a little more than his Jewish dignity will justify.

Nor will he question the reasonableness of so doing, although he may not care to spend any logic upon its support. How much more if he be a man who would love his neighbour if he could, will the higher condition unsought have been found in the action! For man is a whole; and so soon as he *unites himself* by obedient action, the truth that is in him makes itself known to him, shining from the new whole. For his action is his

183

response to his maker's design, his individual part in the creation of himself, his yielding to the All in all, to the tides of whose harmonious cosmoplastic life all his being thenceforward lies open for interpenetration and assimilation. When will once begins to aspire, it will soon find that action must precede feeling, that the man may know the foundation itself of feeling.

With those who recognize no authority as the ground of tentative action, a doubt, a suspicion of truth, ought to be ground enough for putting it to the test.

The End of the Divine Education

The whole system of divine education as regards the relation of man and man, has for its end that a man should love his neighbour as himself. It is not a lesson that he can learn by itself, or a duty the obligation of which can be shown by argument, any more than the difference between right and wrong can be defined in other terms than their own.

"But that difference," it may be objected, "manifests itself of itself to every mind: it is self-evident; whereas the loving of one's neighbour is *not* seen to be a primary truth; so far from it, that far the greater number of those who hope for an eternity of blessedness through him who taught it, do not really believe it to be a truth; believe, on the contrary, that the paramount obligation is to take care of one's self at much risk of forgetting one's neighbour."

But the human race generally has got as far as the recognition of right and wrong; and therefore most men are born capable of making the distinction. The race has not yet lived long enough for its latest offspring to be born with the perception of the truth of love to the neighbour. It is to be seen by the present individual only after a long reception of and submission to the education of life. And once seen, it is believed.

Love for God and Love for Man

The whole constitution of human society exists for the express end, I say, of teaching the two truths by which man lives, love to God and love to man. I will say nothing more of the mysteries of the parental relation, because they belong to the teaching of the former truth, than that we come into the world as we do, to look up to the love over us, and see in it a symbol, poor and weak, yet the best we can have or receive of the divine love.* And thousands more would find it easy to love God if they had not such miserable types of him in the self-seeking, impulse-driven, purposeless, faithless beings who are all they have for father and mother, and to whom their children are no dearer than her litter is to the unthinking dam.

What I want to speak of now, with regard to the second great commandment, is the relation of brotherhood and sisterhood. Why does my brother come of the same father and mother? Why do I behold the helplessness and confidence of his infancy? Why is the infant laid on the knee of the child? Why do we grow up with the same nurture? Why do we behold the wonder of the sunset and the mystery of the growing moon together? Why do we share one bed, join in the same games, and attempt the same exploits? Why do we quarrel, vow revenge and silence and endless enmity, and, unable to resist the brotherhood within us, wind arm in arm and forget all within the hour?

Is it not that love may grow lord of all between him and me? Is it not that I may feel towards him what there are no words or forms of words to express—a love

---

*It might be expressed after a deeper and truer fashion by saying that, God making human affairs after his own thoughts, they are therefore such as to be the best teachers of love to him and love to our neighbour. This is an immeasurably nobler and truer manner of regarding them than as a scheme or plan invented by the divine intellect.

namely, in which the divine self rushes forth in utter self-forgetfulness to live in the contemplation of the brother—a love that is stronger than death,—glad and proud and satisfied?

But if love stop there, what will be the result? Ruin to itself; loss of the brotherhood. He who loves not his brother for deeper reasons than those of a common parentage will cease to love him at all. The love that enlarges not its borders, that is not ever spreading and including, and deepening, will contract, shrivel, decay, die. I have had the sons of my mother that I may learn the universal brotherhood. For there is a bond between me and the most wretched liar that ever died for the murder he would not even confess, closer infinitely than that which springs only from having one father and mother. That we are the sons and the daughters of God born from his heart, the outcoming offspring of his love, is a bond closer than all other bonds in one. No man ever loved his own child aright who did not love him for his humanity, for his divinity, to the utter forgetting of his origin from himself. The son of my mother is indeed my brother by this greater and closer bond as well; but if I recognize that bond between him and me at all, I recognize it for my race.

True, and thank God! the greater excludes not the less; it makes all the weaker bonds stronger and truer, nor forbids that where all are brothers, some should be those of our bosom. Still my brother according to the flesh is my first neighbour, that we may be very nigh to each other, whether we will or no, while our hearts are tender, and so may learn *brotherhood*. For our love to each other is but the throbbing of the heart of the great brotherhood, and could come only from the eternal Father, not from our parents.

Then my second neighbour appears, and who is he? Whom I come in contact with soever. He with whom I have any transactions, any human dealings whatever. Not the man only with whom I dine; not the friend only with whom I share my thoughts; not the man only whom my compassion would lift from some slough; but the man who makes my clothes; the man who prints my book; the man who drives me in his cab: the man who begs from me in the street, to whom, it may be, for brotherhood's sake, I must not give; yea, even the man who condescends to me.

With all and each there is a chance of doing the part of a neighbour, if in no other way yet by speaking truly, acting justly, and thinking kindly. Even these deeds will help to that love which is born of righteousness. All true action clears the springs of right feeling, and lets their waters rise and flow. A man must not choose his neighbour; he must take the neighbour that God sends him. In him, whoever he be, lies, hidden or revealed, a beautiful brother. The neighbour is just the man who is next to you at the moment, the man with whom any business has brought you in contact.

Loving the Other

Thus will love spread and spread in wider and stronger pulses till the whole human race will be to the man sacredly lovely. Drink-debased, vice-defeatured, pride-puffed, wealth-bollen, vanity-smeared, they will yet be brothers, yet be sisters, yet be God-born neighbours. Any rough-hewn semblance of humanity will at length be enough to move the man to reverence and affection. It is harder for some to learn thus than for others. There are those whose first impulse is ever to repel and not to receive. But learn they may, and learn they must. Even these may grow in this grace until a countenance unknown will awake in them a yearning of (affection rising to pain), because there is for it no expression, and they can only give the man to God and be still.

And now will come in all the arguments out of which the man tried in vain before to build a stair up to the sunny heights of love. "Ah brother! thou hast a soul like mine," he will say. "Out of thine eyes thou lookest, and sights and sounds and odours visit thy soul as mine, with wonder and tender comforting. Thou too lovest the faces of thy neighbours. Thou art oppressed with thy sorrows, uplifted with thy joys. Perhaps thou knowest not so well as I, that a region of gladness surrounds all thy grief, of light all thy darkness, of peace all thy tumult. Oh, my brother! I will love thee. I cannot come very near thee: I will love thee the more. It may be thou dost not love thy neighbour; it may be thou thinkest only how to get from him, how to gain by him. How lonely then must thou be! how shut up in thy poverty-stricken room, with the bare walls of thy selfishness, and the hard couch of thy unsatisfaction! I will love thee the more. Thou shalt not be alone with thyself. Thou art not me; thou art another life—a second self; therefore I can, may, and will love thee."

When once to a man the human face is the human face divine, and the hand of his neighbour is the hand of a brother, then will he understand what St. Paul meant when he said, "I could wish that myself were accursed from Christ for my brethren." But he will no longer understand those who, so far from feeling the love of their neighbour an essential of their being, expect to be set free from its law in the world to come. There, at least, for the glory of God, they may limit its expansive tendencies to the narrow circle of their heaven. On its battlements of safety, they will regard hell from afar, and say to each other, "Hark! Listen to their moans. But do not weep, for they are our neighbours no more."

St. Paul would be wretched before the throne of God, if he thought there was one man beyond the pale of his mercy, and that as much for God's glory as for the man's sake. And what shall we say of the man Christ Jesus? Who, that loves his brother, would not, upheld by the love of Christ, and with a dim hope that in the far-off time there might be some help for him, arise from the company of the blessed, and walk down into the dismal regions of despair, to sit with the last, the only unredeemed, the Judas of his race, and be himself more blessed in the pains of hell, than in the glories of heaven?

Who, in the midst of the golden harps and the white wings, knowing that one of his kind, one miserable brother in the old-world-time when men were taught to love their neighbour as themselves, was howling unheeded far below in the vaults of the creation, who, I say, would not feel that he must arise, that he had no choice, that, awful as it was, he must gird his loins, and go down into the smoke and the darkness and the fire, travelling the weary and fearful road into the far country to find his brother?—who, I mean, that had the mind of Christ, that had the love of the Father?

But it is a wild question. God is, and shall be, all in all. Father of our brothers and sisters! thou wilt not be less glorious than we, taught of Christ, are able to think thee. When thou goest into the wilderness to seek, thou wilt not come home until thou hast found. It is because we hope not for them in thee, not knowing thee, not knowing thy love, that we are so hard and so heartless to the brothers and sisters whom thou hast given us.

Life Is in Loving

One word more: This love of our neighbour is the only door out of the dungeon of self, where we mope and mow, striking sparks, and rubbing phosphorescences out of the walls, and blowing our own breath in our own nostrils, instead of issuing to the fair sunlight of God, the sweet winds of the universe. The man thinks his consciousness is himself; whereas his life consisteth in the inbreathing of God, and the consciousness of the universe of truth. To have himself, to know himself, to enjoy himself, he calls life; whereas, if he would forget himself, tenfold would be his life in God and his neighbours.

The region of man's life is a spiritual region. God, his friends, his neighbours, his brothers all, is the wide world in which alone his spirit can find room. Himself is his dungeon. If he feels it not now, he will yet feel it one day—feel it as a loving soul would feel being prisoned in a dead body, wrapped in sevenfold cerements, and buried in a stone-ribbed vault within the last ripple of the sound of the chanting people in the church above.

His life is not in knowing that he lives, but in loving all forms of life. He is made for the All, for God, who is the All, is his life. And the essential joy of his life lies abroad in the liberty of the All. His delights, like those of the Ideal Wisdom, are with the sons of men. His health is in the body of which the Son of man is the head. The whole region of life is open to him—nay, he must live in it or perish.

Nor thus shall a man lose the consciousness of well-being. Far deeper and more complete, God and his neighbour will flash it back upon him—pure as life. No more will he agonize "with sick assay" to generate it in the light of his own decadence. For he shall know the glory of his own being in the light of God and of his brother.

But he may have begun to love his neighbour, with the hope of ere long loving him as himself, and notwithstanding start back affrighted at yet another word of our Lord, seeming to be another law yet harder than the first, although in truth it is not another, for without obedience to it the former cannot be attained unto. He has not yet learned to love his neighbour as himself whose heart sinks within him at the word, *I say unto you, Love your enemies.*

CHAPTER SEVEN

The God of the Living

He is not a God of the dead, but of the living;
for all live unto him (Luke 20:38).

Christer and the Sadducees

It is a recurring cause of perplexity in our
Lord's teaching, that he is too simple for us; that while
we are questioning with ourselves about the design of
Solomon's carving upon some gold-plated door of the
temple, he is speaking about the foundations of Mount
Zion, yea, of the earth itself, upon which it stands. If the
reader of the Gospel supposes that our Lord was here
using a verbal argument with the Sadducees, namely, "I
am the God of Abraham, Isaac, and Jacob; therefore they
are," he will be astonished that no Sadducee was found
with courage enough to reply: "All that God meant was
to introduce himself to Moses as the same God who had
aided and protected his fathers while they were alive,
saying, I am he that was the God of thy fathers. They
found me faithful. Thou, therefore, listen to me, and thou
too shalt find me faithful *unto* the death."

But no such reply suggested itself even to the Sadducees of that day, for their eastern nature could see argument beyond logic. Shall God call himself the God of the

dead, of those who were alive once, but whom he either could not or would not keep alive? Is that the Godhood, and its relation to those who worship it? The changeless God of an ever-born and ever-perishing torrent of life; of which each atom cries with burning heart, *My God!* and straightway passes into the Godless cold! "Trust in me, for I took care of your fathers once upon a time, though they are gone now. Worship and obey me, for I will be good to you for threescore years and ten, or thereabouts; and after that, when you are not, and the world goes on all the same without you, I will call myself your God still." God changes not. Once God he is always God. If he has once said to a man, "I am thy God, and that man has died the death of the Sadducee's creed," then we have a right to say that God is the God of the dead.

"And wherefore should he not be so far the God of the dead, if during the time allotted to them here, he was the faithful God of the living?" What God-like relation can the ever-living, life-giving, changeless God hold to creatures who partake not of his life, who have death at the very core of their being, are not worth their Maker's keeping alive? To let his creatures die would be to change, to abjure his Godhood, to cease to be that which he had made himself. If they are not worth keeping alive, then his creating is a poor thing, and he is not so great, nor so divine as even the poor thoughts of those his dying creatures have been able to imagine him.

But our Lord says, "All live unto him." With Him death is not. Thy life sees our life, O Lord. All of whom *all* can be said, are present to thee. Thou thinkest about us, eternally more than we think about thee. The little life that burns within the body of this death, glows unquenchable in thy true-seeing eyes. If thou didst forget us for a moment then indeed death would be. But unto thee we live. The beloved pass from our sight, but they pass not from thine. This that we call death, is but a form in the eyes of men. It looks something final, an awful cessation, an utter change. It seems not probable that there is anything beyond. But if God could see us before we were, and make us after his ideal, that we shall have passed from the eyes of our friends can be no argument that he beholds us no longer.

"All live unto Him." Let the change be ever so great, ever so imposing; let the unseen life be ever so vague to our conception, it is not against reason to hope that God could see Abraham, after his Isaac had ceased to see him; saw Isaac after Jacob ceased to see him; saw Jacob after some of the Sadducees had begun to doubt whether there ever had been a Jacob at all. He remembers them; that is, he carries them in his mind: he of whom God thinks, lives. He takes to himself the name of *Their God*. The Living One cannot name himself after the dead; when the very Godhead lies in the giving of life. Therefore they must be alive. If he speaks of them, remembers his own loving thoughts of them, would he not have kept them alive if he could; and if he could not, how could he create them? Can it be an easier thing to call into life than to keep alive?

"But if they live to God, they are aware of God. And if they are aware of God, they are conscious of their own being: Whence then the necessity of a resurrection?"

The Resurrection of the Body

For their relation to others of God's children in mutual revelation; and for fresh revelation of God to all.—But let us inquire what is meant by the resurrection of the body. "With what body do they come?"

Surely we are not required to believe that the same body is raised again. That is against science, common sense, Scripture. St. Paul represents the matter quite otherwise. One feels ashamed of arguing such a puerile point. Who could wish his material body which has indeed died over and over again since he was born, never remaining for one hour composed of the same matter, its endless activity depending upon its endless change, to be fixed as his changeless possession, such as it may then be, at the moment of death, and secured to him in worthless identity for the ages to come?

A man's material body will be to his consciousness at death no more than the old garment he throws aside at night, intending to put on a new and a better in the morning. To desire to keep the old body seems to me to argue a degree of sensual materialism excusable only in those pagans who in their Elysian fields could hope to possess only such a thin, fleeting, dreamy, and altogether funebrial existence, that they might well long for the thicker, more tangible bodily being in which they had experienced the pleasures of a tumultuous life on the upper world. As well might a Christian desire that the hair which has been shorn from him through all his past life should be restored to his risen and glorified head.

Yet not the less is the doctrine of the Resurrection gladdening as the sound of the silver trumpet of its visions, needful as the very breath of life to our longing souls. Let us know what it means, and we shall see that it is thus precious.

The Camera of God's Revelation

Let us first ask what is the use of this body of ours. It is the means of revelation to us, the *camera* in which God's eternal shows are set forth. It is by the body that we come into contact with nature, with our fellow-men, with all their revelations of God to us. It is through the body that we receive all the lessons of passion, of suffering, of love, of beauty, of science. It is through the body that we are both trained outwards from ourselves, and driven inwards into our deepest selves to find God. There is glory and might in this vital evanescence, this slow glacier-like flow of clothing and revealing matter, this ever uptossed rainbow of tangible humanity. It is no less of God's making than the spirit that is clothed therein.

We cannot yet have learned all that we are meant to learn through the body. How much of the teaching even of this world can the most diligent and most favoured man have exhausted before he is called to leave it! Is all that remains to be lost? Who that has loved this earth can but believe that the spiritual body of which St. Paul speaks will be a yet higher channel of such revelation?

The meek who have found that their Lord spake true, and have indeed inherited the earth, who have seen that all matter is radiant of spiritual meaning, who would not cast a sigh after the loss of mere animal pleasure, would, I think, be the least willing to be without a body, to be unclothed without being again clothed upon. Who, after centuries of glory in heaven, would not rejoice to behold once more that patient-headed child of winter and spring, the meek snowdrop? In whom, amidst the golden choirs, would not the vision of an old sunset wake such a song as the ancient dwellers of the earth would with gently flattened palm hush their throbbing harps to hear?

All this revelation, however, would render only *a* body necessary, not this body. The fulness of the word *resurrection* would be ill met if this were all. We need not only a body to convey revelation to us, but a body to reveal us to others. The thoughts, feelings, imaginations which arise in us, must have their garments of revelation whereby shall be made manifest the unseen world within us to our brothers and sisters around us; else is each left in human loneliness.

Now, if this be one of the uses my body served on earth before, the new body must be like the old. Nay, it must be the same body, glorified as we are glorified, with all that was distinctive of each from his fellows more visible than ever before. The accidental, the nonessential, the unrevealing, the incomplete will have vanished. That which made the body what it was in the eyes of those who loved us will be tenfold there. Will not this be the resurrection of the body? of the same body though not of the same dead matter?

Every eye shall see the beloved; every heart will cry, "My own again!—more mine because more himself than ever I beheld him!" For do we not say on earth, "He is not himself to-day," or "She looks her own self" or "She is more like herself than I have seen her for long"? And is not this when the heart is glad and the face is radiant? For we carry a better likeness of our friends in our hearts than their countenances, save at precious seasons, manifest to us.

The Resurrection and the Restoration of Fellowship

Who will dare to call anything less than this a resurrection? Oh, how the letter killeth! There are those who can believe that the dirt of their bodies will rise the same as it went down to the friendly grave, who yet doubt if they will know their friends when they rise again. And they call *that* believing in the resurrection!

What! shall a man love his neighbour as himself, and must he be content not to know him in heaven? Better be content to lose our consciousness, and know ourselves no longer. What! shall God be the God of the families of the earth, and shall the love that he has thus created towards father and mother, brother and sister, wife and child, go moaning and longing to all eternity; or worse, far worse, die out of our bosoms? Shall God be God, and shall this be the end?

Ah, my friends! what will resurrection or life be to me, how shall I continue to love God as I have learned to love him through you, if I find he cares so little for this human heart of mine, as to take from me the gracious visitings of your faces and forms? True, I might have a gaze at Jesus, now and then; but he would not be so good as I had thought him. And how should I see him if I could not see you? God will not take you, has not taken you from me to bury you out of my sight in the abyss of his own unfathomable being, where I cannot follow and find you, myself lost in the same awful gulf. No, our God is an unveiling, a revealing God. He will raise you from the dead, that I may behold you; that that which vanished from the earth may again stand forth, looking out of the same eyes of eternal love and truth, holding out the same mighty hand of brotherhood, the same delicate and gentle, yet strong hand of sisterhood, to me, this me that knew you and loved you in the days gone by.

I shall not care that the matter of the forms I loved a thousand years ago has returned to mingle with the sacred goings on of God's science, upon that far-off world wheeling its nursery of growing loves and wisdoms through space; I shall not care that the muscle which now sends the ichor through your veins is not formed of the very particles which once sent the blood to the pondering brain, the flashing eye, or the nervous right arm; I shall not care, I say, so long as it is yourselves that are before me, beloved; so long as through these forms I know that I look on my own, on my loving souls of the ancient time; so long as my spirits have got garments of revealing after their own old lovely fashion, garments to reveal themselves to me.

The new shall then be dear as the old, and for the same reason, that it reveals the old love. And in the changes which, thank God, must take place when the mortal puts on immortality, shall we not feel that the nobler our friends are, the more they are themselves; that the more the idea of each is carried out in the perfection of beauty, the more like they are to what we thought them in our most exalted moods, to that which we saw in them in the rarest moments of profoundest communion, to that which we beheld through the veil of all their imperfections when we loved them the truest?

Lord, evermore give us this resurrection, like thine own in the body of thy Transfiguration. Let us see, and hear, and know, and be seen, and heard, and known, as thou seest, hearest, and knowest. Give us glorified bodies through which to reveal the glorified thoughts which shall then inhabit us, when not only shalt thou reveal God, but each of us shall reveal thee.

And for this, Lord Jesus, come thou, the child, the obedient God, that we may be one with thee, and with every man and woman whom thou hast made, in the Father.

❧

"Life" is taken from the second series of MacDonald's Unspoken Sermons, *published in 1886. " 'More life!' is the unconscious prayer of all creation. . . ." This is Mac-Donald's message, and when men say they are tired of life or are discontented what they really mean is that they do not have enough of life. This life that we long for is nothing less than God Himself. Only by uniting our will with God's, by being conformed to the Being of our origins, can we truly have life.*

CHAPTER EIGHT

Life

"I came that they may have life, and may have
it abundantly" (John 10:10).

More Life

In a word, He came to supply all our lack—
from the root outward; for what is it we need but more
life? What does the infant need but more life? What does
the bosom of his mother give him but life in abundance?
What does the old man need, whose limbs are weak and
whose pulse is low, but more of the life which seems ebb-
ing from him? Weary with feebleness, he calls upon
death, but in reality it is life he wants. It is but the en-
croaching death in him that desires death. He longs for
rest, but death cannot rest; death would be as much an
end to rest as to weariness: even weakness cannot rest; it
takes strength as well as weariness to rest.

How different is the weariness of the strong man after
labour unduly prolonged, from the weariness of the sick
man who in the morning cries out, "Would God it were
evening!" and in the evening, "Would God it were morning!" Low-sunk life imagines itself weary of life, but it is

death, not life, it is weary of. Never a cry went out after the opposite of life from any soul that knew what life is. Why does the poor, worn, outworn suicide seek death? Is it not in reality to escape from death?—from the death of homelessness and hunger and cold; the death of failure, disappointment, and distraction; the death of the exhaustion of passion; the death of madness—of a household he cannot rule; the death of crime and fear of discovery? He seeks the darkness because it seems a refuge from the death which possesses him. He is a creature possessed by death; what he calls his life is but a dream full of horrible phantasms.

"More life!" is the unconscious prayer of all creation, groaning and travailing for the redemption of its lord, the son who is not yet a son. Is not the dumb cry to be read in the faces of some of the animals, in the look of some of the flowers, and in many an aspect of what we call Nature?

The Difficulty of God's Creation

All things are possible with God, but all things are not easy. It is easy for him *to be*, for there he has to do with his own perfect will: it is not easy for him to create—that is, after the grand fashion which alone will satisfy his glorious heart and will, the fashion in which he is now creating us. In the very nature of being—that is, God—it must be hard—and divine history shows how hard—to create that which shall be not himself, yet like himself. The problem is, so far to separate from himself that which must yet on him be ever and always and utterly dependent, that it shall have the existence of an individual, and be able to turn and regard him—choose him, and say, "I will arise and go to my Father," and so develop in itself the highest *divine* of which it is capable— the will for the good against the evil—the will to be one

with the life whence it has come, and in which it still is—
the will to close the round of its procession in its return,
so working the perfection of reunion—to shape in its
own life the ring of eternity—to live immediately, consciously, and active-willingly from its source, from its
own very life—to restore to the beginning the end that
comes of that beginning—to be the thing the maker
thought of when he willed, ere he began to work its
being.

I imagine the difficulty of doing this thing, of effecting
this creation, this separation from himself such that will
in the creature shall be possible—I imagine, I say, the
difficulty of such creation so great, that for it God must
begin inconceivably far back in the infinitesimal regions
of beginnings—not to say before anything in the least
resembling man, but eternal miles beyond the last
farthest-pushed discovery in *protoplasm*—to set in motion that division from himself which in its grand result
should be individuality, consciousness, choice, and conscious choice—choice at last pure, being the choice of
the right, the true, the divinely harmonious. Hence the
final end of the separation is not individuality; that is
but a means to it; the final end is oneness—an impossibility without it. For there can be no unity, no delight of
love, no harmony, no good in being, where there is but
one. Two at least are needed for oneness; and the greater
the number of individuals, the greater, the lovelier, the
richer, the diviner is the possible unity.

God's Sacrificial Creation

God is life, and the will-source of life. In the outflow-
ing of that life, I know him; and when I am told that he is
love, I see that if he were not love he would not, could not
create. I know nothing deeper in him than love, nor believe there is in him anything deeper than love—nay, that

there can be anything deeper than love. The being of God is love, therefore creation. I imagine that from all eternity he has been creating. As he saw it was not good for man to be alone, so has he never been alone himself;—from all eternity the Father has had the Son, and the never-begun existence of that Son I imagine an easy outgoing of the Father's nature; while to make other beings—beings like us, I imagine the labour of a God, an eternal labour.

Speaking after our poor human fashions of thought—the only fashions possible to us—I imagine that God has never been contented to be alone even with the Son of his love, the prime and perfect idea of humanity, but that he has from the first willed and laboured to give existence to other creatures who should be blessed with his blessedness—creatures whom he is now and always has been developing into likeness with that Son—a likeness for long to be distant and small, but a likeness to be for ever growing: perhaps never one of them yet, though unspeakably blessed, has had even an approximate idea of the blessedness in store for him.

Let no soul think that to say God undertook a hard labour in willing that many sons and daughters should be sharers of the divine nature, is to abate his glory! The greater the difficulty, the greater is the glory of him who does the thing he has undertaken—without shadow of compromise, with no half-success, but with a triumph of absolute satisfaction to innumerable radiant souls! He knew what it would cost!—not energy of will alone, or merely that utterance and separation from himself which is but the first of creation, though that may well itself be pain—but sore suffering such as we cannot imagine, and could only be God's, in the bringing out, call it birth or development, of the God-life in the individual soul—a suffering still renewed, a labour thwarted ever by that soul itself, compelling him to take, still at the cost of suffering, the not absolutely best, only the best possible means left him by the resistance of his creature.

Man finds it hard to get what he wants, because he does not want the best; God finds it hard to give, because he would give the best, and man will not take it. What Jesus did, was what the Father is always doing; the suffering he endured was that of the Father from the foundation of the world, reaching its climax in the person of his Son. God provides the sacrifice; the sacrifice is himself. He is always, and has ever been, sacrificing himself to and for his creatures. It lies in the very essence of his creation of them.

The worst heresy, next to that of dividing religion and righteousness, is to divide the Father from the Son—in thought or feeling or action or intent; to represent the Son as doing that which the Father does not himself do. Jesus did nothing but what the Father did and does. If Jesus suffered for men, it was because his Father suffers for men; only he came close to men through his body and their senses, that he might bring their spirits close to his Father and their Father, so giving them life, and losing what could be lost of his own. He is God our Savior: it is because God is our Savior that Jesus is our Savior. The God and Father of Jesus Christ could never possibly be satisfied with less than giving himself to his own!

The unbeliever may easily imagine a better God than the common theology of the country offers him; but not the lovingest heart that ever beat can even reflect the length and breadth and depth and height of that love of God which shows itself in his Son—one, and of one mind, with himself. The whole history is a divine agony to give divine life to creatures. The outcome of that agony, the victory of that creative and again creative energy, will be radiant life, whereof joy unspeakable is the flower. Every child will look in the eyes of the Father, and the eyes of the Father will receive the child with an infinite embrace.

The Only Reality Is Life

The life the Lord came to give us is a life exceeding that of the highest undivine man, by far more than the life of that man exceeds the life of the animal the least human. More and more of it is for each who will receive it, and to eternity. The Father has given to the Son to have life in himself; that life is our light. We know life only as light; it is the life in us that makes us see. All the growth of the Christian is the more and more life he is receiving. At first his religion may hardly be distinguishable from the mere prudent desire to save his soul; but at last he loses that very soul in the glory of love, and so saves it; self becomes but the cloud on which the white light of God divides into harmonious unspeakable.

"In the midst of life we are in death," said one; it is more true that in the midst of death we are in life. Life is the only reality; what men call death is but a shadow—a word for that which cannot be—a negation, owing the very idea of itself to that which it would deny. But for life there could be no death. If God were not, there would not even be nothing. Not even nothingness preceded life. Nothingness owes its very idea to existence.

One form of the question between matter and spirit is, which was first, and caused the other—things or thoughts; whether things without thought caused thought, or thought without things caused things. To those who cannot doubt that thought was first, causally preceding the earliest material show, it is easily plain that death can be the cure for nothing, that the cure for everything must be life—that the ills which come with existence, are from its imperfection, not of itself—that what we need is more of it. We who *are*, have nothing to do with death; our relations are alone with life. The thing that can mourn can mourn only from lack; it cannot mourn because of being, but because of not enough being. We are vessels of life, not yet full of the wine of life; where the wine does not reach, there the clay cracks, and aches, and is distressed. Who would therefore pour out the wine that is there, instead of filling to the brim with more wine!

All the being must partake of essential being; life must be assisted, upheld, comforted, every part, with life. Life is the law, the food, the necessity of life. Life is everything. Many doubtless mistake the joy of life for life itself; and, longing after the joy, languish with a thirst at once poor and inextinguishable; but even that thirst points to the one spring. These love self, not life, and self is but the shadow of life. When it is taken for life itself, and set as the man's centre, it becomes a live death in the man, a devil he worships as his god; the worm of the death eternal he clasps to his bosom as his one joy!

The soul compact of harmonies has more life, a larger being, than the soul consumed of cares; the sage is a larger life than the clown; the poet is more alive than the man whose life flows out that money may come in; the man who loves his fellow is infinitely more alive than he whose endeavour is to exalt himself above him; the man who strives to be better, than he who longs for the praise of the many; but the man to whom God is all in all, who feels his life-roots hid with Christ in God, who knows himself the inheritor of all wealth and worlds and ages, yea, of power essential and in itself, that man has begun to be alive indeed.

Our One Lack Is Life

Let us in all the troubles of life remember—that our one lack is life—that what we need is more life—more of the life-making presence in us making us more, and more largely, alive. When most oppressed, when most weary of life, as our unbelief would phrase it, let us bethink ourselves that it is in truth the inroad and presence of death we are weary of. When most inclined to sleep, let us rouse ourselves to live. Of all things let us avoid the false refuge of a weary collapse, a hopeless yielding to things as they are. It is the life in us that is discontented; we need more of what is discontented, not more of the cause of its discontent.

Discontent, I repeat, is the life in us that has not enough of itself, is not enough to itself, so calls for more. He has the victory who, in the midst of pain and weakness, cries out, not for death, not for the repose of forgetfulness, but for strength to fight; for more power, more consciousness of being, more God in him; who, when sorest wounded, says with Sir Andrew Barton in the old ballad:—

> Fight on my men, says Sir Andrew Barton,
>   I am hurt, but I am not slain;
> I'll lay me down and bleed awhile,
>   And then I'll rise and fight again;

—and that with no silly notion of playing the hero—what have creatures like us to do with heroism who are not yet barely honest!—but because so to fight is the truth, and the only way.

If, in the extreme of our exhaustion, there should come to us, as to Elijah when he slept in the desert, an angel to rouse us, and show us the waiting bread and water, how would we carry ourselves? Would we, in faint unwillingness to rise and eat, answer, "Lo I am weary unto death! The battle is gone from me! It is lost, or unworth gaining! The world is too much for me! Its forces will not heed me! They have worn me out! I have wrought no salvation even for my own, and never should work any, were I to live for ever! It is enough; let me now return whence I came; let me be gathered to my fathers and be at rest!"? I should be loth to think that, if the enemy, in recognizable shape, came roaring upon us, we would not, like the red-cross knight, stagger, heavy sword in nerveless arm, to meet him; but, in the feebleness of foiled effort, it wants yet more faith to rise and partake of the food that shall bring back more effort, more travail, more weariness.

The true man trusts in a strength which is not his, and which he does not feel, does not even always desire; believes in a power that seems far from him, which is yet at the root of his fatigue itself and his need of rest—rest as far from death as is labour. To trust in the strength of God in our weakness; to say, "I am weak: so let me be: God is strong;" to seek from him who is our life, as the natural, simple cure of all that is amiss with us, power to do, and be, and live, even when we are weary,—this is the victory that overcometh the world.

To believe in God our strength in the face of all seeming denial, to believe in him out of the heart of weakness and unbelief, in spite of numbness and weariness and lethargy; to believe in the wide-awake real, through all the stupefying, enervating, distorting dream; to will to wake, when the very being seems athirst for a godless repose;—these are the broken steps up to the high fields where repose is but a form of strength, strength but a form of joy, joy but a form of love. "I am weak," says the true soul, "but not so weak that I would not be strong; not so sleepy that I would not see the sun rise; not so lame but that I would walk! Thanks be to him who perfects strength in weakness, and gives to his beloved while they sleep!"

If we will but let our God and Father work his will

with us, there can be no limit to his enlargement of our existence, to the flood of life with which he will overflow our consciousness. We have no conception of what life might be, of how vast the consciousness of which we could be made capable. Many can recall some moment in which life seemed richer and fuller than ever before; to some, such moments arrive mostly in dreams: shall soul, awake or asleep, infold a bliss greater than its Life, the living God, can seal, perpetuate, enlarge? Can the human twilight of a dream be capable of generating or holding a fuller life than the morning of divine activity?

Surely God could at any moment give to a soul, by a word to that soul, by breathing afresh into the secret caves of its being, a sense of life before which the most exultant ecstasy of earthly triumph would pale to ashes! If ever sunlit, sail-crowded sea, under blue heaven flecked with wind-chased white, filled your soul as with a new gift of life, think what sense of existence must be yours, if he whose thought has but fringed its garment with the outburst of such a show, take his abode with you, and while thinking the gladness of a God inside your being, let you know and feel that he is carrying you as a father in his bosom!

God Is Life

I have been speaking as if life and the consciousness of it were one; but the consciousness of life is not life; it is only the outcome of life. The real life is that which is of and by itself—is life because it wills itself—which *is*, in the active, not the passive sense: this can only be God. But in us there ought to be a life correspondent to the life that is God's; in us also must be the life that wills itself— a life in so far resembling the self-existent life and partaking of its image, that it has a share in its own being. There is an original act possible to the man, which must initiate the reality of his existence. He must live in and by willing to live.

A tree lives; I hardly doubt it has some vague consciousness, known by but not to itself, only to the God who made it; I trust that life in its lowest forms is on the way to thought and blessedness, is in the process of that separation, so to speak, from God, in which consists the creation of living souls; but the life of these lower forms is not life in the high sense—in the sense in which the word is used in the Bible: true life knows and rules itself; the eternal life is life come awake. The life of the most exalted of the animals is not such whatever it may become, and however I may refuse to believe their fate and being fixed as we see them.

But as little as any man or woman would be inclined to call the existence of the dog, looking strange lack out of his wistful eyes, an existence to be satisfied with—his life an end sufficient in itself, as little could I, looking on the human pleasure, the human refinement, the common human endeavour around me, consent to regard them as worthy the name of life. What in them is true dwells amidst an unchallenged corruption, demanding repentance and labour and prayer for its destruction. The condition of most men and women seems to me a life in death, an abode in unwhited sepulchres, a possession of withering forms by spirits that slumber, and babble in their dreams.

That they do not feel it so is nothing. The sow wallowing in the mire may rightly assert it her way of being clean, but theirs is not the life of the God-born. The day must come when they will hide their faces with such shame as the good man yet feels at the memory of the time when he lived like them.

There is nothing for man worthy to be called life, but the life eternal—God's life, that is, after his degree shared by the man made to be eternal also. For he is in the image of God, intended to partake of the life of the most high, to be alive as he is alive. Of this life the outcome and the light is righteousness, love, grace, truth; but the life itself is a thing that will not be defined, even as God will not be defined: it is a power, the formless cause of form. It has no limits whereby to be defined. It shows itself to the soul that is hungering and thirsting after righteousness, but that soul cannot show it to another, save in the shining of its own light.

The ignorant soul understands by this life eternal only an endless elongation of consciousness; what God means by it is a being like his own, a being beyond the attack of decay or death, a being so essential that it has no relation whatever to nothingness; a something which is, and can never go to that which is not, for with that it never had to do, but came out of the heart of life, the heart of God, the fountain of being; an existence partaking of the divine nature, and having nothing in common, any more than the Eternal himself, with what can pass or cease: God owes his being to no one, and his child has no lord but his Father.

Oneness with God

This life, this eternal life, consists for man in absolute oneness with God and all divine modes of being, oneness with every phase of right and harmony. It consists in a love as deep as it is universal, as conscious as it is unspeakable; a love that can no more be reasoned about than life itself—a love whose presence is its all-sufficing proof and justification, whose absence is an annihilating defect: he who has it not cannot believe in it: how should death believe in life, though all the birds of God are singing jubilant over the empty tomb! The delight of such a being, the splendour of a consciousness rushing from the wide open doors of the fountain of existence, the ecstasy of the spiritual sense into which the surge of life essential, immortal, increate, flows in silent fulness from the heart of hearts—what may it, what must it not be, in the great day of God and the individual soul!

What then is our practical relation to the life original? What have we to do towards the attaining to the resurrection from the dead? If we did not make, could not have made ourselves, how can we, now we are made, do anything at the unknown roots of our being? What relation of conscious unity can be betwixt the self-existent God, and beings who live at the will of another, beings who could not refuse to be—cannot even cease to be, but must, at the will of that other, go on living, weary of what is not life, able to assert their relation to life only by refusing to be content with what is not life?

The self-existent God is that other by whose will we live; so the links of the unity must already exist, and can but require to be brought together. For the link in our being wherewith to close the circle of immortal oneness with the Father, we must of course search the deepest of man's nature: there only, in all assurance, can it be found. And there we do find it. For the *will* is the deepest, the strongest, the divinest thing in man; so, I presume, is it in God, for such we find it in Jesus Christ.

Here, and here only, in the relation of the two wills, God's and his own, can a man come into vital contact— on the eternal idea, in no one-sided unity of completest dependence, but in willed harmony of dual oneness— with the All-in-all. When a man can and does entirely say, "Not my will, but thine be done"—when he so wills the will of God as to do it, then is he one with God—one, as a true son with a true father. When a man wills that his being be conformed to the being of his origin, which is the life in his life, causing and bearing his life, therefore absolutely and only of its kind, one with it more and deeper than words or figures can say—to the life which is itself, only more of itself, and more than itself, causing itself—when the man thus accepts his own causing life, *and sets himself to live the will of that causing life,* humbly eager after the privileges of his origin,—thus receiving God, he becomes, in the act, a partaker of the divine nature, a true son of the living God, and an heir of all he possesses: by the obedience of a son, he receives into himself the very life of the Father. Obedience is the joining of the links of the eternal round. Obedience is but the other side of the creative will. Will is God's will, obedience is man's will; the two make one.

The root-life, knowing well the thousand troubles it would bring upon him, has created, and goes on creating other lives, that, though incapable of self-being, they may, by willed obedience, share in the bliss of his essential self-ordained being. If we do the will of God, eternal life is ours—no mere continuity of existence, for that in itself is worthless as hell, but a being that is one with the essential Life, and so within his reach to fill with the abundant and endless outgoings of his love. Our souls shall be vessels ever growing, and ever as they grow, filled with the more and more life proceeding from the Father and the Son, from God the ordaining, and God the obedient.

What the delight of the being, what the abundance of the life he came that we might have, we can never know until we have it. But even now to the holy fancy it may sometimes seem too glorious to support—as if we must die of very life—of more being than we could bear—to awake to a yet higher life, and be filled with a wine which our souls were heretofore too weak to hold! To be for one moment aware of such pure simple love towards but one of my fellows as I trust I shall one day have towards each, must of itself bring a sense of life such as the utmost effort of my imagination can but feebly shadow now—a mighty glory of consciousness!—not to be always present, indeed, for my love, and not my glory in that love, is my life.

There would be, even in that one love, in the simple purity of a single affection such as we were created to generate, and intended to cherish, towards all, an expansion of life inexpressible, unutterable. For we are made for love, not for self. Our neighbour is our refuge; *self* is our demon-foe. Every man is the image of God to every man, and in proportion as we love him, we shall know the sacred fact. The precious thing to human soul is, and one day shall be known to be, every human soul. And if it be so between man and man, how will it not be betwixt the man and his Maker, between the child and his eternal Father, between the created and the creating Life? Must not the glory of existence be endlessly redoubled in the infinite love of the creature—for all love is infinite—to the infinite God, the great one life, than whom is no other—only shadows, lovely shadows of him!

Reader to whom my words seem those of inflation and foolish excitement, it can be nothing to thee to be told that I seem to myself to speak only the words of truth and soberness; but what if the cause why they seem other to thy mind be—not merely that thou art not whole, but that thy being nowise thirsts after harmony, that thou art not of the truth, that thou hast not yet begun to live? How should the reveller, issuing worn and wasted from the haunts where the violent seize joy by force to find her perish in their arms—how should such reveller, I say, break forth and sing with the sons of the morning, when the ocean of light bursts from the fountain of the east? As little canst thou, with thy mind full of petty cares, or still more petty ambitions, understand the groaning and travailing of the creation. It may indeed be that thou art honestly desirous of saving thy own wretched soul, but as yet thou canst know but little of thy need of him who is *the first and the last and the living one*.

꒲

In 1870 MacDonald published a volume titled The Miracles of Our Lord. *In the "Introduction" MacDonald briefly outlines why he does not find miracles difficult to accept. Christ's miracles are simply a natural outcome of His being united to God the Father through obedience.*

One of the classes that MacDonald divides Christ's miracles into is those of "The Government of Nature." These miracles are easy for MacDonald to accept because if God visited men in the form of man "he would naturally show himself Lord over their circumstances." To the objection that some might pose that the laws of God should not change, MacDonald answers that what we perceive to be a breach of God's laws is not so to God. In all of these miracles Christ showed that nature and all of creation was subject to the Father.

CHAPTER NINE

The Miracles of Our Lord: Introduction

I have been requested to write some papers on our Lord's miracles. I venture the attempt in the belief that, seeing they are one of the modes in which his unseen life found expression, we are bound through them to arrive at some knowledge of that life. For he has come, The Word of God, that we may know God: every word of his then, as needful to the knowing of himself, is needful to the knowing of God, and we must understand, as far as we may, every one of his words and every one of his actions, which, with him, were only another form of word. I believe this the immediate end of our creation. And I believe that this will at length result in the unravelling for us of what must now, more or less, appear to every man the knotted and twisted coil of the universe.

Belief in the Miracles

It seems to me that it needs no great power of faith to believe in the miracles—for true faith is a power, not a mere yielding. There are far harder things to believe than the miracles. For a man is not required to believe in them save as believing in Jesus. If a man can believe that there is a God, he may well believe that, having made creatures capable of hungering and thirsting for him, he must be capable of speaking a word to guide them in their feeling after him. And if he is a grand God, a God worthy of being God, yea (his metaphysics even may show the seeker), if he is a God capable of being God, he will speak the clearest grandest word of guidance which he can utter intelligible to his creatures.

For us, that word must simply be the gathering of all the expressions of his visible works into an infinite human face, lighted up by an infinite human soul behind it, namely, that potential essence of man, if I may use a word of my own, which was in the beginning with God. If God should *thus* hear the cry of the noblest of his creatures, for such are all they who do cry after him, and in very deed show them his face, it is but natural to expect that the deeds of the great messenger should be just the works of the Father done in little. If he came to reveal his Father in miniature, as it were (for in these unspeakable things we can but use figures, and the homeliest may be the holiest), to tone down his great voice, which, too loud for men to hear it aright, could but sound to them as an inarticulate thundering, into such a still small voice as might enter their human ears in welcome human speech, then the words that his Father does so widely, so grandly that they transcend the vision of men, the Son must do briefly and sharply before their very eyes.

This, I think, is the true nature of the miracles, an epitome of God's processes in nature beheld in immediate connection with their source—a source as yet lost to the eyes and too often to the hearts of men in the far-receding gradations of continuous law. That men might

see the will of God at work, Jesus did the works of his
Father thus.

Objections to the Miracles

Here I will suppose some honest, and therefore hon-
ourable, reader objecting: But do you not thus place the
miracles in dignity below the ordinary processes of nature? I answer: The miracles are mightier far than any
goings on of nature as beheld by common eyes, dissociat-
ing them from a living will; but the miracles are surely
less than those mighty goings on of nature with God beheld at their heart. In the name of him who delighted to
say "My Father is greater than I," I will say that his miracles in bread and in wine were far less grand and less
beautiful than the works of the Father they represented,
in making the corn to grow in the valleys, and the grapes
to drink the sunlight on the hill-sides of the world, with
all their infinitudes of tender gradation and delicate
mystery of birth. But the Son of the Father be praised,
who, as it were, condensed these mysteries before us,
and let us see the precious gifts coming at once from gracious hands—hands that love could kiss and nails could
wound.

There are some, I think, who would perhaps find it
more possible to accept the New Testament story if the
miracles did not stand in the way. But perhaps, again, it
would be easier for them to accept both if they could
once look into the true heart of these miracles. So long
as they regard only the surface of them, they will, most
likely, see in them only a violation of the laws of nature:
when they behold the heart of them, they will recognize
there at least a possible fulfilment of her deepest laws.

With such, however, is not my main business now, any
more than with those who cannot believe in a God at all,

and therefore to whom a miracle is an absurdity. I may, however, just make this one remark with respect to the latter—that perhaps it is better they should believe in no God than believe in such a God as they have yet been able to imagine. Perhaps thus they are nearer to a true faith—except indeed they prefer the notion of the unconscious generating the conscious, to that of a self-existent love, creative in virtue of its being love. Such have never loved woman or child save after a fashion which has left them content that death should seize on the beloved and bear them back to the maternal dust. But I doubt if there can be any who thus would choose a sleep-walking Pan before a wakeful Father. At least, they cannot know the Father and choose the Pan.

The Works of the Son Are the Works of the Father

Let us then recognize the works of the Father as epitomized in the miracles of the Son. What in the hands of the Father are the mighty motions and progresses and conquests of life, in the hands of the Son are miracles. I do not myself believe that he valued the working of these miracles as he valued the utterance of the truth in words; but all that he did had the one root, *obedience*, in which alone can any son be free. And what is the highest obedience? Simply a following of the Father—a doing of what the Father does. Every true father wills that his child should be as he is in his deepest love, in his highest hope. All that Jesus does is of his Father. What we see in the Son is of the Father. What his works mean concerning him, they mean concerning the Father.

Much as I shrink from the notion of a formal shaping out of design in any great life, so unlike the endless freedom and spontaneity of nature (and He is the Nature of nature), I cannot help observing that his first miracle was one of creation—at least, is to our eyes more like creation than almost any other—for who can say that it was creation, not knowing in the least what creation is, or what was the process in this miracle?

CHAPTER TEN

The Government of Nature

The miracles I include in this class are the following:

1. The turning of water into wine, already treated of, given by St. John.
2. The draught of fishes, given by St. Luke.
3. The draught of fishes, given by St. John.
4. The feeding of the four thousand, given by St. Matthew and St. Mark.
5. The feeding of the five thousand, recorded by all the Evangelists.
6. The walking on the sea, given by St. Matthew, St. Mark, and St. John.
7. The stilling of the storm, given by St. Matthew, St. Mark, and St. Luke.
8. The fish bringing the piece of money, told by St. Matthew alone.

The Nature of These Miracles

These miracles, in common with those already considered, have for their end the help or deliverance of man.

They differ from those, however, in operating mediately, through a change upon external things, and not at once on their human objects.

But besides the fact that they have to do with what we call nature, they would form a class on another ground. In those cases of disease, the miracles are for the setting right of what has gone wrong, the restoration of the order of things,—namely, of the original condition of humanity. No doubt it is a law of nature that where there is sin there should be suffering; but even its cure helps to restore that righteousness which is highest nature; for the cure of suffering must not be confounded with the absence of suffering.

But the miracles of which I have now to speak, show themselves as interfering with what we may call the righteous laws of nature. Water should wet the foot, should ingulf him who would tread its surface. Bread should come from the oven last, from the field first. Fishes should be now here now there, according to laws ill understood of men—nay, possibly according to a piscine choice quite unknown of men. Wine should take ripening in the grape and in the bottle. In all these cases it is otherwise.

Yet even in these, I think, the restoration of an original law—the supremacy of righteous man, is foreshown. While a man cannot order his own house as he would, something is wrong in him, and therefore in his house. I think a true man should be able to rule winds and waters and loaves and fishes, for he comes of the Father who made the house for him. Had Jesus not been capable of these things, he might have been the best of men, but either he could not have been a perfect man, or the perfect God, if such there were, was not in harmony with the perfect man. Man is not master in his own house because he is not master in himself, because he is not a law unto himself—is not himself obedient to the law by

which he exists. Harmony, that is law, alone is power.
Discord is weakness. God alone is perfect, living, self-
existent law.

A Defense of These Miracles

I will try, in a few words, to give the ground on which I
find it possible to accept these miracles. I cannot lay it
down as for any other man. I do not wonder at most of
those to whom the miracles are a stumbling-block. I do a
little wonder at those who can believe in Christ and yet
find them a stumbling-block.

How God creates, no man can tell. But as man is made
in God's image, he may think about God's work, and dim
analogies may arise out of the depth of his nature
which have some resemblance to the way in which
God works. I say then, that, as we are the offspring of
God—the children of his will, like as the thoughts move
in a man's mind, we live in God's mind. When God thinks
anything, then that thing *is*. His thought of it is its life.
Everything is because God thinks it into being. Can it
then be very hard to believe that he should alter by a
thought any form or appearance of things about us?

"It is inconsistent to work otherwise than by law."

True; but we know so little of this law that we cannot
say what is essential in it, and what only the so far irregular consequence of the unnatural condition of those for
whom it was made, but who have not yet willed God's
harmony. We know so little of law that we cannot certainly say what would be an infringement of this or that
law. That which at first sight appears as such, may be
but the operating of a higher law which rightly domi-
nates the other. It is the law, as we call it, that a stone
should fall to the ground. A man may place his hand beneath the stone, and then *if his hand be strong enough*, it
is the law that the stone shall not fall to the ground. The

law has been lawfully prevented from working its full end.

In similar ways, God might stop the working of one law by the intervention of another. Such intervention, if not understood by us, would be what we call a miracle. Possibly a different condition of the earth, producible according to law, might cause everything to fly off from its surface instead of seeking it. The question is whether or not we can believe that the usual laws might be set aside by laws including higher principles and wider operations. All I have to answer is—Give me good reason, and I can. A man may say—"What seems good reason to you, does not to me." I answer, "We are both accountable to that being, if such there be, who has lighted in us the candle of judgment. To him alone we stand or fall. But there must be a final way of right, towards which every willing heart is led,—and which no one can find who does not seek it."

All I want to show here, is a conceivable region in which a miracle might take place without any violence done to the order of things. Our power of belief depends greatly on our power of imagining a region in which the things might be. I do not see how some people *could* believe what to others may offer small difficulty. Let us beware lest what we call faith be but the mere assent of a mind which has cared and thought so little about the objects of its so-called faith, that it has never seen the difficulties they involve. Some such believers are the worst antagonists of true faith—the children of the Pharisees of old.

Harmony with a Higher Law

If any one say we ought to receive nothing of which we have no experience; I answer, there is in me a necessity, a desire before which all my experience shrivels into a mockery. Its complement must lie beyond. We ought, I grant, to accept nothing for which we cannot see the probability of some sufficient reason, but I thank God that this sufficient reason is not for me limited to the realm of experience. To suppose that it was, would change the hope of a life that might be an ever-burning sacrifice of thanksgiving, into a poor struggle with events and things and chances—to doom the Psyche to perpetual imprisonment in the worm. I desire the higher; I care not to live for the lower. The one would make me despise my fellows and recoil with disgust from a self I cannot annihilate; the other fills me with humility, hope, and love. Is the preference for the one over the other foolish then—even to the meanest judgment?

A higher condition of harmony with law, may one day enable us to do things which must now *appear* an interruption of law. I believe it is in virtue of the absolute harmony in him, his perfect righteousness, that God can create at all. If man were in harmony with this, if he too were righteous, he would inherit of his Father a something in his degree correspondent to the creative power in Him; and the world he inhabits, which is but an extension of his body, would, I think, be subject to him in a way surpassing his wildest dreams of dominion, for it would be the perfect dominion of holy law—a virtue flowing to and from him through the channel of a perfect obedience.

I suspect that our Lord in all his dominion over nature, set forth only the complete man—man as God means him one day to be. Why should he not know where the fishes were? or even make them come at his will? Why should not that will be potent as impulse in them? If we admit what I hail as the only fundamental idea upon which I can speculate harmoniously with facts, and as alone disclosing regions wherein contradictions are soluble, and doubts previsions of loftier truth—I mean the doctrine of the Incarnation; or if even we admit that Jesus was good beyond any other goodness we know, why should it not seem possible that the whole region of inferior things might be more subject to him than to us? And if more, why not altogether? I believe that some of these miracles were the natural result of a physical nature perfect from the indwelling of a perfect soul, whose unity with the Life of all things and in all things was absolute—in a word, whose sonship was perfect.

These Miracles Reveal the Father

If in the human form God thus visited his people, he would naturally show himself Lord over their circumstances. He will not lord it over their minds, for such lordship is to him abhorrent: they themselves must see and rejoice in acknowledging the lordship which makes them free. There was no grand display, only the simple doing of what at the time was needful. Some say it is a higher thing to believe of him that he took things just as they were, and led the revealing life without the aid of wonders. On any theory this is just what he did as far as his own life was concerned. But he had no ambition to show himself the best of men. He comes to reveal the Father. He will work even wonders to that end, for the sake of those who could not believe as he did and had to be taught it.

No miracle was needful for himself: he saw the root of the matter—the care of God. But he revealed this root in a few rare and hastened flowers to the eyes that could not see to the root. There is perfect submission to lower law for himself, but revelation of the Father to them by the introduction of higher laws operating in the upper regions bordering upon ours, not separated from ours by an impassable gulf—rather connected by gently ascending stairs, many of whose gradations he could blend in one descent. He revealed the Father as being *under* no law, but as law itself, and the cause of the laws we know—the cause of all harmony because himself *the* harmony.

Men had to be delivered not only from the fear of suffering and death, but from the fear, which is a kind of worship, of nature. Nature herself must be shown subject to the Father and to him whom the Father had sent. Men must believe in the great works the Father through the little works of the Son: all that he showed was little to what God was doing. They had to be helped to see that it was God who did such things as often as they were done. He it is who causes the corn to grow for man. He gives every fish that a man eats. Even if things are terrible yet they are God's, and the Lord will still the storm for their faith in Him—tame a storm, as a man might tame a wild beast—for his Father measures the waters in the hollow of his hand, and men are miserable not to know it. For himself, I repeat, his faith is enough; he sleeps on his pillow nor dreams of perishing.

The Government of the Animal Kingdom

On the individual miracles of this class, I have not much to say. The first of them was wrought in the animal kingdom.

He was teaching on the shore of the lake, and the people crowded him. That he might speak with more freedom, he stepped into an empty boat, and having prayed Simon the owner of it, who was washing his nets near by, to thrust it a little from the shore, sat down, and no longer incommoded by the eagerness of his audience, taught them from the boat. When he had ended he told Simon to launch out into the deep, and let down his nets for a draught. Simon had little hope of success, for there had been no fish there all night; but he obeyed, and caught such a multitude of fishes that the net broke. They had to call another boat to their aid, and both began to sink from the overload of fishes.

But the great marvel of it wrought on the mind of Simon as every wonder tends to operate on the mind of an honest man: it brought his sinfulness before him. In self-abasement he fell down at Jesus' knees. Whether he thought of any individual sins at the moment, we cannot tell; but he was painfully dissatisfied with himself. He knew he was not what he ought to be. I am unwilling however to believe that such a man desired, save, it may be, as a passing involuntary result of distress, to be rid of the holy presence. I judge rather that his feeling was like that of the centurion—that he felt himself unworthy to have the Lord in his boat. He may have feared that the Lord took him for a good man, and his honesty could not endure such a mistake: "Depart from me, for I am a sinful man, O Lord."

The Lord accepted the spirit, therefore *not* the word of his prayer.

"Fear not; from henceforth thou shalt catch men."

His sense of sinfulness, so far from driving the Lord from him, should draw other men to him. As soon as that cry broke from his lips, he had become fit to be a fisher of men. He had begun to abjure that which separated man from man.

After his resurrection, St. John tells us the Lord appeared one morning, on the shore of the lake, to some of his disciples, who had again been toiling all night in vain. He told them once more how to cast their net, and they were not able to draw it for the multitude of fishes.

"It is the Lord," said St. John, purer-hearted, perhaps therefore keener-eyed, than the rest.

Since the same thing had occurred before, Simon had

become the fisher of men, but had sinned grievously against his Lord. He knew that Lord so much better now, however, than when he heard it was he, instead of crying *Depart from me,* he cast himself into the sea to go to him.

The Miraculous Feedings

I take next the feeding of the four thousand with the seven loaves and the few little fishes, and the feeding of the five thousand with the five loaves and the two fishes. Concerning these miracles, I think I have already said almost all I have to say. If he was the Son of God, the bread might as well grow in his hands as the corn in the fields. It is, I repeat, only a doing in condensed form, hence one more easily associated with its real source, of that which God is for ever doing more widely, more slowly, and with more detail both of fundamental wonder and of circumstantial loveliness. Whence more fittingly might food come than from other hands of such an elder brother?

No doubt there will always be men who cannot believe it:—happy are they who demand a good reason, and yet can believe a wonder! Associated with words which appeared to me foolish, untrue, or even poor in their content, I should not believe it. Associated with such things as he spoke, I can receive it with ease, and I cherish it with rejoicing.

It must be noted in respect of the feeding of the five thousand, that while the other evangelists merely relate the deed as done for the necessities of the multitude, St. John records also the use our Lord made of the miracle. It was the outcome of his essential relation to humanity. Of humanity he was ever the sustaining food. To humanity he was about to give himself in an act of such utter devotion as could only be shadowed—not in the spoken, afterwards in the acted symbol of the eucharist.

The miracle was a type of his life as the life of the world, a sign that from him flows all the weal of his creatures. The bread we eat is but its outer husk: the true bread is the Lord himself, to have whom in us is eternal life. "Except ye eat the flesh of the Son of man and drink his blood ye have no life in you." He knew that the grand figure would disclose to the meditation of the loving heart infinitely more of the truth of the matter than any possible amount of definition and explanation, and yet must ever remain far short of setting forth the holy fact to the boldest and humblest mind.

But lest they should start upon a wrong track for the interpretation of it, he says to his disciples afterwards, that this body of his should return to God; that what he had said concerning the eating of it had a spiritual sense: "It is the spirit that giveth life; the flesh profiteth nothing"—for that. In words he contradicts what he said before, that they might see the words to have meant infinitely more than as words they were able to express; that not their bodies on his body, but their souls must live on his soul, by a union and communion of which the eating of his flesh and the drinking of his blood was, after all, but a poor and faint figure.

In this miracle, for the souls as for the bodies of men, he did and revealed the work of the Father. He who has once understood the meaning of Christ's words in connection with this miracle, can never be content they should be less than true concerning his Father in heaven. Whoever would have a perfect Father, must believe that he bestows his very being for the daily food of his creatures. He who loves the glory of God will be very jealous of any word that would enhance his greatness by representing him incapable of suffering. Verily God has taken and will ever take and endure his share, his largest share of that suffering in and through which the whole creation groans for the sonship.

Christ's Walking on the Water

Follows at once the equally wonderful story of his walking on the sea to the help of his disciples. After the former miracle, the multitude would have taken him by force to make him their king. Any kind of honour they would readily give him except that obedience for the truth's sake which was all he cared for. He left them and went away into a mountain alone to pray to his Father. Likely he was weary in body, and also worn in spirit for lack of that finer sympathy which his disciples could not give him being very earthly yet. He who loves his fellows and labours among those who can ill understand him will best know what this weariness of our Lord must have been like. He had to endure the world-pressure of surrounding humanity in all its ungodlike phases.

Hence even he, the everlasting Son of the Father, found it needful to retire for silence and room and comfort into solitary places. There his senses would be free, and his soul could the better commune with the Father. The mountain-top was his chamber, the solitude around him its closed door, the evening sky over his head its open window. There he gathered strength from the will of the Father for what yet remained to be done for the world's redemption. How little could the men below, who would have taken him by force and made him a king, understand of such communion! Yet every one of them must go hungering and thirsting and grasping in vain, until the door of that communion was opened for him. They would have made him a king: he would make them poor in spirit, mighty in aspiration, all kings and priests unto God.

But amidst his prayer, amidst the eternal calm of his

rapturous communion, he saw his disciples thwarted by a wind stronger than all their rowing: he descended the hill and walked forth on the water to their help.

If ignorant yet devout speculation may be borne with here, I venture to say that I think the change of some kind that was necessary somehow before the body of the Son of Man could, like the Spirit of old, move upon the face of the waters, passed, not upon the water, but, by the will of the Son of Man himself, upon his own body. I shall have more to say concerning this in a following chapter—now I merely add that we know nothing yet, or next to nothing, of the relation between a right soul and a healthy body.

To some no doubt the notion of a healthy body implies chiefly a perfection of all the animal functions, which is, on the supposition, a matter of course; but what I should mean by an absolutely healthy body is, one entirely under the indwelling spirit, and responsive immediately to all the laws of its supremacy, whatever those laws may be in the divine ideal of a man. As we are now, we find the diseased body tyrannizing over the almost helpless mind: the healthy body would be the absolutely obedient body. What power over his own dwelling a Savior coming fresh from the closest speech with him who made that body for holy subjection, might have, who can tell!

If I hear of any reasonable wonder resulting therefrom, I shall not find it hard to believe, and shall be willing to wait until I, pure, inhabit an obedient house, to understand the plain thing which is now a mystery. Meantime I can honour the laws I do know, and which honest men tell me they have discovered, no less than those honest men who—without my impulse, it may be, to speculate in this direction—think such as I foolish in employing the constructive faculty with regard to these things.

But where, I pray them, lies any field so absolutely its

region as the unknown which yet the heart yearns to know? Such cannot be the unknowable. It is endless comfort to think of something that *might* be true. And the essence of whatever seems to a human heart to be true, I expect to find true—in greater forms, and without the degrading accidents which so often accompany it in the brain of the purest thinker. Why should I not speculate in the only direction in which things to me worthy of speculation appear likely to lie?

There is a wide *may be* around us; and every true speculation widens the probability of changing the *may be* into the *is*. The laws that are known and the laws that shall be known are all lights from the Father of lights: he who reverently searches for such will not long mistake a flash in his own brain for the candle of the Lord. But if he should mistake, he will be little the worse, so long as he is humble, and ready to acknowledge error; while, if he should be right, he will be none the worse for having seen the glimmer of the truth from afar—may, indeed, come to gather a little honour from those who, in the experimental verification of an idea, do not altogether forget that, without some foregone speculation, the very idea on which they have initiated their experiment, and are now expending their most valued labour, would never have appeared in their firmament to guide them to new facts and realities.

Nor would it be impossible to imagine how St. Peter might come within the sphere of the holy influence, so that he, too, for a moment should walk on the water. Faith will yet prove itself as mighty a power as it is represented by certain words of the Lord which are at present a stumbling-block even to devout Christians, who are able to accept them only by putting explanations upon them which render them unworthy of his utterance. When I say *a power,* I do not mean in itself, but as connecting the helpless with the helpful, as uniting the empty need with the full supply, as being the conduit through which it is right and possible for the power of the creating God to flow to the created necessity.

When the Lord got into the boat, the wind ceased, "and immediately," says St. John, "the ship was at the land whither they went." As to whether the ceasing of the wind was by the ordinary laws of nature, or some higher law first setting such in operation, no one who has followed the spirit of my remarks will wonder that I do not care to inquire: they are all of one. Nor, in regard to their finding themselves so quickly at the end of their voyage, will they wonder if I think that we may have just one instance of space being subject to the obedient God, and that his wearied disciples, having toiled and rowed hard for so long, might well find themselves at their desired haven as soon as they received him into their boat.

Either God is all in all, or he is nothing. Either Jesus is the Son of the Father, or he did no miracle. Either the miracles are fact, or I lose—not my faith in this man— but certain outward signs of truths which these very signs have aided me to discover and understand and see in themselves.

The Stilling of the Storm

The miracle of the stilling of the storm naturally follows here.

Why should not he, who taught his disciples that God numbered the very hairs of their heads, do what his Father is constantly doing—still storms—bring peace out of uproar? Of course, if the storm was stilled, it came about by natural causes—that is, by such as could still a storm. That anything should be done by unnatural causes, that is, causes not of the nature of the things concerned, is absurd.

The sole question is whether nature works alone, as

some speculators think, or whether there is a soul in her, namely, an intent;—whether these things are the result of thought, or whether they spring from a dead heart; unconscious, yet productive of conscious beings, to think, yea, speculate eagerly concerning a conscious harmony hinted at in their broken music and conscious discord; beings who, although thus born of unthinking matter, invent the notion of an all lovely, perfect, self-denying being, whose thought gives form to matter, life to nature, and thought to man—subjecting himself for their sakes to the troubles their waywardness has brought upon them, that they too may at length behold a final good—may see the Holy face to face—think his thoughts and will his wisdom!

That things should go by a law which does not recognize the loftiest in him, a man feels to be a mockery of him. There lies little more satisfaction in such a condition of things than if the whole were the fortuitous result of ever conflicting, never combining forces. Wherever individual and various necessity, choice, and prayer, come in, there must be the present God, able and ready to fit circumstances to the varying need of the thinking, willing being he has created.

Machinery will not do here—perfect as it may be. That God might make a world to go on with absolute physical perfection to all eternity, I could easily believe; but where the gain?—nay, where the fitness, if he would train thinking beings to his own freedom? For such he must be ever present, ever have room to order things for their growth and change and discipline and enlightenment. The present living idea informing the cosmos, is nobler than all forsaken perfection—nobler, as a living man is nobler than an automaton.

If one should say: "The laws of God ought to admit of no change," I answer: The same working of unalterable laws might under new circumstances *look* a breach of those laws. That God will never alter his laws, I fully admit and uphold, for they are the outcome of his truth and fact; but that he might not act in ways unrecognizable by us as consistent with those laws, I have yet to see reason ere I believe. Why should his perfect will be limited by our understanding of that will? Should he be paralyzed because we are blind? That he should ever require us to believe of him what we think wrong, I do not believe; that he should present to our vision what may be inconsistent with our half-digested and constantly changing theories, I can well believe. Why not—if only to keep us from petrifying an imperfect notion, and calling it an *Idea?*

What I would believe is, that a present God manages the direction of those laws, even as a man, in his inferior way, works out his own will in the midst and by means of those laws. Shall God create that which shall fetter and limit and enslave himself? What should his laws, as known to us, be but the active mode in which he embodies certain truths—that mode also the outcome of his own nature? If so, they must be always capable of falling in with any, if not of effecting every, expression of his will.

The Fish with Money in Its Mouth

There remains but one miracle of this class to consider—one to some minds involving greater difficulties than all the rest. They say the story of the fish with a piece of money in its mouth is more like one of the tales of eastern fiction than a sober narrative of the quiet-toned gospel. I acknowledge a likeness: why might there not be some likeness between what God does and what man invents?

But there is one noticeable difference: there is nothing of colour in the style of the story. No great roc, no valley of diamonds, no earthly grandeur whatever is hinted at in the poor bare tale. Peter had to do with fishes every day of his life: an ordinary fish, taken with the hook, was here the servant of the Lord—and why should not the poor fish have its share in the service of the Master? Why should it not show for itself and its kind that they were utterly his? that along with the waters in which they dwelt, and the wind which lifteth up the waves thereof, they were his creatures, and gladly under his dominion?

What the scaly minister brought was no ring, no rich jewel, but a simple piece of money, just enough, I presume, to meet the demand of those whom, although they had no legal claim, our Lord would not offend by a refusal; for he never cared to stand upon his rights, or treat that as a principle which might be waived without loss of righteousness. I take for granted that there was no other way at hand for those poor men to supply the sum required of them.

God's Words to His Children *(1887) is a collection of MacDonald's sermons from diverse sources. In "The Only Freedom," which was originally published in* The English Pulpit To-Day, *MacDonald speaks of a slavery that is liberty. Freedom lies in obedience, for Christ Himself was free because of His complete devotion to the will of the Father. Freedom means acting like God out of the essence of our nature and choosing good with our whole hearts.*

"The Resurrection Harvest," which also appears in God's Words to His Children, *originally appeared in MacDonald's 1868 novel* The Seaboard Parish. *MacDonald sees that this world is full of resurrections. The sun enacts a resurrection every night and day, and we ourselves "die" every night to rise every morning. In the seasons of the earth and in the animal world there are also resurrections. All of these are dim shadows of the resurrection into life that we shall have, a resurrection out of evil and into good that begins even in this life.*

ॐ

CHAPTER ELEVEN

The Only Freedom

"Paul, a servant of Jesus Christ" (Rom. 1:1).

The Meaning of "Servant"

St. Paul, in addressing the Romans, begins thus: "Paul, a servant of Jesus Christ." Well, you all know that it is more than that that he says. I do not know why they put the word "bondservant" in the margin. For my part, I should translate it just as it stands, "Paul, a slave of Jesus Christ." And again—for he does not want to be exclusive even in this humility—when he is writing to the Philippians, he joins another with him, namely, Timothy, his young friend, and he says, "Paul and Timothy, slaves of Jesus Christ." But the word does mean just that. It is not what we call a servant in our day, for they could not come and go as they pleased. They were not even servants who were slaves taken in war, but it means even more than the bondslave. It means a born slave, and there we have it—"a born slave of Jesus Christ."

It is a figure, you know; but the plague of it is that most people, who deal with the figures in the New Testament, make them to mean less because they are figures. That is the way in which the commonplace devil that possesses many men and women makes them treat all the high and holy things. Where there is a figure used in the New Testament, it means more than it can say; and more than any word that man can utter did St. Paul mean when he said that he was a born slave of Jesus Christ.

No doubt there is in the word an element which St. Paul did not mean—did not feel. You know how a mother will sometimes, just out of tenderness to her child, call it bad names. So St. Paul here, just in the despair of faith, takes delight in belonging to Christ utterly, altogether, inconceivably, saved by Christ himself, for he could not tell or feel—he knew that he could not even feel—how much he belonged to Christ; and he used a word that indicates in it something which is not real, not true. He says, "I am the slave of Jesus Christ," and yet, if any man in this world was free besides the Lord himself, that man was St. Paul.

As for us, as soon as we begin to say high things in our human speech, we immediately begin to say them wrong. There is no help for it. Whatever of high things can be put into words is not right; it is not correct. We are only trying after what language is unequal to. It cannot do all, and therefore sometimes we just go wrong the other way, and use, as it were, the wrong word in a kind of agony of outreaching after the true.

Paul the Enthusiast

"But St. Paul was an enthusiast." Yes, I believe that he was an enthusiast; and, if he had not been an enthusiast about such a thing as this, he would not have been worthy to be a slave to the lowest of Christ's people. There is no reality in the relation of things that are high, if we be not enthusiastic about them, if they do not possess us, hold us, fill us, lead us, drive us, teach us, feed us, live in us, and make us live in them. No good can be done without enthusiasm. There is no reality of love without enthusiasm.

What! shall I know anything at all that is genuine about Jesus Christ? Am I a fool capable of believing that that man came from the bosom of the Father to be to me my loving Brother and my Savior; to take me, at his own torture, out of my misery, out of myself, which is my torture, into the life of his Father in heaven? Shall I believe that—shall I even believe that he had not a selfish thought in him, and not be enthusiastic about him? Have I the faculty of enthusiasm in me? Is it possible for me to give myself away—to do anything that is not urged and suggested by the lower self? Am I capable of these things at all?

Then, if I am not enthusiastic about Jesus Christ, this whole faculty of my nature lies useless, rotting in me, for there is nothing else in the universe to call it out, or capable of calling it out. The poor enthusiasms that one sees in the world for things that are less than the truth, or that are small passing facts of our condition here—look how they last when a man is vigorous, and how they wither when he grows older! But you will find that St. Paul, at the very last of his life, was more a slave of Jesus Christ than ever before—far more his slave than when he lay struck blind and helpless by the light of his appearing.

For my part, it seems to me a grand proof—and we can have no external proof better, though we may have better proof in ourselves, for the least feeling of these things in ourselves is a higher and better proof than anything brought from the outside—I say that the fact that a man like St. Paul, (brought up as he was, with such a brain and such a heart, and turned the wrong way at first,) should be capable of burning with such enthusiasm for a man of whose history he knew very little that was real or true until he saw him in heavenly glory—that after that he should live to be the rejoicing slave of Jesus Christ—is it a wonder that such a fact should weigh with me ten times more than the denial of the highest intellect of this world who gives me by the very terms that he uses, concerning what he thinks my faith, the conviction that he knows nothing about what I believe? He talks as if he did, but he knows nothing about it. St. Paul knew the Lord Christ; and, therefore, heart and soul, mind, body, and brain, he belonged to Jesus Christ, even as his born slave.

Slavery That Is a Liberty

But let us try to understand a little what is meant by a slavery which is a liberty. One of the first feelings of the noble-minded youth is a love of liberty. In our history he has been taught it from his earliest thought, and he feels that the grand thing is that he shall be free and the slave of no man. As a rule he has a very low notion of what liberty is, and in most cases it does not grow very much better as he gets older; but still there is, at the root of it, a something genuine and real, which is capable of being interpreted into a high and holy thing.

But is it, as the boy thinks about it? Well, it is just to do as he likes; or, if he carries it a little higher, and thinks of political liberty, it is that nobody may meddle with him, that he is to stand without any weight, or bond, or command upon him. And for the sake of this kind of liberty, too often, he will bind his soul in chains of misery. Sometimes, for instance, he will run away from school; he will run away from home; he will shirk doing the things that his parents tell him; and, in order that his feet may be free to wander where they will, he ties up his inner man in a sense of wrath, in garments of pain, in a feeling of bondage; and because he would be free he makes himself a slave far deeper than any outward law could make him.

Suppose, however, that there was no law of parent, or teacher, or magistrate, or ruler of any kind whatever, laid upon us, and suppose that the man has plenty of money and all kinds of what he calls freedom to go and do what he pleases. Suppose that, outside, he is aware of no bondage whatever. That cannot last long. As soon as there comes a touch of pain, the least sense of weakness—as soon as the first white begins to come on the hair—well, perhaps not quite so soon as that, but when he has the first feeling, "I am not quite capable of what I used to do,"—as soon as any of these merest touches come on the consciousness of a man, the sense of freedom begins to go.

But suppose that in the heyday of a man's strength, in the heartiness of ripe youth, before middle age has begun to come, he can move as he pleases and do as he wills, and suppose that there is no one to say nay to him, is he free? Young man, would you think that that was all right? Would you think that this was your calling? Would you say, "For this end came I into the world, that I might do whatever I liked"? And would you feel that you were grand and free? If you do feel so, you will not believe me, but I tell you—and one day you will believe me if you remember it, which is not likely—I tell you that, to me and to every man who has had the experience of any effort of true liberty, you are a most wretched slave, for your very ideal is slavery; your very high notion is mean and despicable.

You cannot see it; I know that, but you do not see everything yet; and the time is coming when you will be compelled to see it, and can no more help seeing it than now you can help—or, rather, I should say, will help not seeing it. For what is it that drives you on? There is a devil who has whispered to you—affected, perhaps, a certain convolution of your brain, touched you at some certain spot; and you say that you are free, and all the time you are the real sport of temptation. You call it liberty. You stay till the point of the arrow that directs you turns against you and pierces you to the centre. You stay till the devil that tempted you mocks you, and you gaze at him and get no help; for there is no such thing in the world as liberty, except under the law of liberty; that is, the acting according to the essential laws of our own being—not our feelings which go and come.

The man that will rage one hour and be cold the next—what a fool he is if he supposes that he is to walk either by his rage or by his coldness! It is a law that he is to obey. He is to follow the lines upon which this being of his is constructed, this central, original, heart-emotion of his existence. Why, as soon might a man attempt to drive some great engine backward—as soon might he lay hold of its centre pinion and try to stop it, as you can think to make it go well with your being if you live contrary to the very essence of your being; for, let me tell you, you are not bad, or, if you are bad, you are damnably bad.

You are not made bad. God forbid; for God made us, and he made nothing bad, and if you will be bad that is fearful indeed. The lines of our being are laid, I will not even say by the hand of the living God, they were laid in his heart. The idea of every one of us was known and thought over in that heart; and, out of his heart we have gone. He has set before us a way that we may turn, and, of our own free will, run back to him, embrace the Father's knees, and be lifted to the Father's heart.

Liberty Lies in Obedience

There is no liberty but in doing right. There is no freedom but in living out of the deeps of our nature—not out of the surface. Why, look at you. You lose your temper.

You think that you are free when you go into a rage. Half-an-hour after you are ashamed. God grant that you may be sorry. That is something more. But you are ashamed of yourself; and yet you think that you are a free man. You acted out the mere surface of your nature—a something which it needed but half-an-hour to make you ashamed of.

That is not liberty. That is acting out of your poor, mean, despicable self, which we have all got, and not out of the divine self, the deepest in us, for the deepest in us is God. We did not come into this world because we willed it. We did not say what we should be. It is God in every man that enables that man even to stretch out his hand. The moment may come when he can lift it no more. Let him will, and will to do it with an agony of willing; yet he cannot raise his hand any more. He cannot do it. It is God; none else.

But I am talking about liberty, and what I want to impress upon those who will be impressed is this—that the one only liberty lies in obedience. Can you lay hold of it? Do you think that Jesus Christ—and he will let me put it so because it is for the sake of the truth—do you think that Jesus Christ would have felt free one moment if he had not been absolutely devoted to the will of his Father in heaven? Suppose it had been possible, which, thank the Lord Christ and his Father, it was not, else we were now in the darkness of helplessness—suppose it had been possible that Jesus Christ should have been less devoted to his Father, for he might have said in the same high, figurative sense that he was the slave of his Father; for, look you, he cares for nothing but his Father's will. There is nothing else that he has anything to do with. The very reason for which he came into the world was "that the world may know that I am of the Father." "As the Father has given me commandment," he says, "so I do;" and then he says, "Arise, let us go hence"—away to the death, because the Father willed it.

Oh, if Jesus had been less the slave of his Father, do you think that he would have felt that he was a free man? Do you not think that that was what made the devil? He had a notion of being free. "Here I am. I will be the slave of no man—not even of the God that made me." And so all goes wrong, and he is the devil—no archangel any longer—and a mean devil, too, who tries to pull all down into the same abyss with himself well knowing that he cannot even give them his pride to uphold them. If, friends, it should be slavery to obey the very source of our being, think what mean creatures we are that, having come from that source, to follow the law of our life is a slavery.

Slaves of Christ

Well, then, we are the born slaves—ah, thank God, we are the born slaves of Christ! But then he is liberty himself, and all his desire is that we should be such noble, true, right creatures that we never can possibly do or think a thing that shall bind a thread round our spirits and make us feel as if we were bound anywhere. He wants us to be free—not as the winds—not to be free as the man who owns no law, but to be free by being law, by being right, by being truth. When you know that the law goes in one way, is it freedom to bring your will against that law, or to avoid it, and go another way, when the very essence of your existence means that you do not oppose, but yield to the conditions—I do not mean arbitrary conditions, but the essential conditions—of your being, those conditions that make your being divine, for God has made us after his own fashion, and when we do as God would do, as God delights to do—when we act according to the divine mind and nature, we are acting according to our own deepest self, which is the law and will of God. Jesus Christ might have said, "I am the slave of my Father in heaven." He has nowhere used the phrase, but it was in that sense that St. Paul said, "I am the slave of Jesus Christ."

Oh, I appeal to you women—I mean those of you that love Jesus Christ—what would you not do to show him that you love him? Then when I say the words there comes a painful thought, whether some of you may not be like children who indulge in all kinds of tender caresses, but who, when told to do something, begin to pout and refuse to obey. Oh, to think that you should love with all your feeling—that you should love the Lord so much, and yet take so little trouble to know from the story left behind what he really now at this moment wants you to do! That is the way to show your love to him.

But, I put it to you again, what would you not do to show that you love him? There were two women who seem to have gone as far as women could go to show their love to him. You know the story—something that one cannot speak. You know the story. Some of you would do that, oh, how rejoicingly! And when you say "Master," you would like to say with St. Paul, just because you have no other word strong enough, "Lord, I am thy bondslave." That was St. Paul's feeling when he used the word. But then St. Paul spent his whole life, all his thoughts, all his energies, simply to obey this Lord and Master; and so he was the one free man—not the only free man; there were some more amongst the apostles, and, by his preaching, here and there and everywhere, there started up free men, or, at least, men who were beginning to grow free by beginning to be the slaves of Jesus Christ.

Willing to Love

But let me show you a little more. I do not say that the moment you begin to obey the Lord Jesus Christ, and to be his slave, then you are free. I do not say that then you know what is meant by liberty. I will show you. There are many things that we know are right, and we are not inclined to do them. There are many things that we know are wrong, and we are inclined to do them. But when the law of liberty comes, the will of Jesus Christ, we begin to try to do the things we do not like to do, and not to do the things that we do like to do.

But do you not see that here is a strife? So long as we are in this condition, so long as we know that we have to do the things that we do not like, and that we must not do the things we would like, we are not free. We are only fighting for freedom, but we are not free. We do not know liberty yet; and yet, on the other hand (try to follow me), if we liked the good things, and did not like the bad thing, and without any thought or effort of our own, just went to the good thing and not to the bad thing, we should not be free either, because we should be going just by the impulse in us.

So there comes a contradiction which it is not easy to explain or understand. But, you know, God could not be satisfied to make us like the animals. A good dog does not bite, because he is not inclined to bite. He loves you, but you do not say that he is high morally because he is not inclined to do anything bad. But if we, choosing, against our liking, to do the right, go on so until we are enabled by doing it to see into the very loveliness and essence of the right, and know it to be altogether beautiful, and then at last never think of doing evil, but delight with our whole souls in doing the will of God, why then, do you not see, we combine the two, and we are free indeed, because we are acting like God out of the essence of our nature, knowing good and evil, and choosing the good with our whole hearts and delighting in it?

It is not enough to love because we cannot help it. We must love, too, because we will it with our whole nature, and then, do you not see, when we come to love one another perfectly, we do not need to be told, "Thou shalt not steal; thou shalt not kill; thou shalt not bear false witness," because the thing is absolutely abhorrent to us, if the thought would come up at all? But, when we have learned to love our neighbor as ourselves the thought of killing and stealing never comes out, or of defrauding or of doing ignoble things and calling them "business." Nothing of that kind. We positively love our neighbor, and to hurt him would be to hurt ourselves worse. That is liberty, but we can come to that only by willing it, the root of our being is that will. We must fall in with it. We must will it ourselves, and then, at last, the lovely will of God will possess us from head to feet and fingers, and we shall live in the very breath of God and act like God himself, free like the Living One, because we are one with the source of our life and our being.

So, friends, you see how all through, as far as the words go, we have got to deal with something like contradictions, but in the meaning of the thing your own hearts tell you—the hearts of many of you, at least, tell you—what it is, and you will see that there is no contradiction in it at all. Though it might be exceedingly difficult to lay it out all plain in logical language, your hearts can understand it. Nay, they witness to it because they have grown hungry. You want to be such children of God as this. You want to be free from the oppression of evil in every way. Nay, the time will come when you will lay down the arms of your battle, fighting for the truth. You will have to lay them down even because you have conquered.

How conquered? Because you are perfectly satisfied with God, one with his will, rejoicing in his joy, living in his life, having no fear, no ambition, no anxiety, but a constant strength of life that death and hell cannot touch. You would not be afraid then if you were cast into the middle of hell fire. The flames could not touch you. If you had a body that they could scorch and burn, yet the soul within you would rise superior even to that torture, because, being of the very nature of God, partakers of the divine nature, you would be able to bear pain in triumph, and with a sense of freedom in the midst of it, and slavery would be far from you.

But I have just a word to say now to those specially who think that they have belonged to Christ for many years. Are you in any sense, can you say it out of your heart and meaning it, "I am a slave of Christ?" Object to the term, and I say, are you the free man of Christ? for they mean the same thing. His slave is his free brother. Is there anything that you do now? And we cannot divide our lives, we cannot say that the private gentleman will be saved when the man of business will be condemned; we are either all Christ's, or not at all, for he has told us that no man can serve two masters.

Are you doing anything now that is not just all that you would like, suppose the thing were to come to be laid open to the purest eyes of those who know you? If there is such a thing as you would not like seen, does the Master see it, or does he not? If he does not, he is no Master; we want a greater. If you think he will let it slip, God forbid that I should serve that Master! I want a Master that will not pass over a farthing, a Master who will not let me go from his cleansing hand even if that hand be washing me with fire so long as there is any spot of defilement on my spirit; and the least shadow of dishonesty is the deepest defilement.

Are you not sometimes content with saying, "I do as my neighbor would do to me"? You cannot say, "I do as I would like my neighbor to do to me," perhaps. I wonder whether you could say, then, what the Lord said; for remember he never said, "Thou shalt love thy neighbor as thyself." That was not what he taught. That was taught long before. The spirit of God taught it, but not by Jesus

Christ. What Christ taught was, "Love one another as I have loved you." Do we behave to our fellow-men as Christ has behaved to us? If we do not, we are not his slaves. We may be even following in the track of his triumph—I do not say that we shall not get in, but I am clear upon this—that we never shall enter until we have passed through what ordeal is needful to make us clean as God himself. We have got to be good, and if we will not willingly of ourselves, he will make us. It is what he made us for, and it ought to be the business of our lives.

O Lord, raise up, we pray thee, thy power, and come among us, and with great might succor us; that whereas, through our sins and wickedness, we are sore let and hindered in running the race that is set before us, thy bountiful grace and mercy may speedily help and deliver us through the satisfaction of thy Son our Lord, to whom, with thee, and the HOLY GHOST, be honor and glory, world without end. *Amen.*

CHAPTER TWELVE

The Resurrection Harvest

*"If by any means I might attain unto the resurrection
of the dead, not as though I had already attained,
either were already perfect"* (Phil. 3:11–12).

The Resurrection of the Sun

The world, my friends, is full of resurrections, and it is not always of the same resurrection that St. Paul speaks. Every night that folds us up in darkness is a death; and those of you that have been out early and have seen the first of the dawn, will know it—the day rises out of the night like a being that has burst its tomb and escaped into life. That you may feel that the sunrise is a resurrection—the word resurrection just means a rising again—I will read you a little description of it from a sermon by a great writer and great preacher called Jeremy Taylor. Listen:

"But as when the sun approaching towards the gates of the morning, he first opens a little eye of heaven and sends away the spirits of darkness, and gives light to a cock, and calls up the lark to matins, and by and by gilds the fringes of a cloud, and peeps over the eastern hills, thrusting out his golden horns like those which decked the brows of Moses, when he was forced to wear a veil, because himself had seen the face of God; and still while a man tells the story, the sun gets up higher, till he shows a fair face and a full light, and then he shines one whole day, under a cloud often, and sometimes weeping great and little showers, and sets quickly; so is a man's reason and his life."

Is not this a resurrection of the day out of the night? Or hear how Milton makes his Adam and Eve praise God in the morning:—

Ye mists and exhalations, that now rise
From hill or steaming lake, dusky or gray,
Till the sun paint your fleecy skirts with gold,
In honor to the world's great Author rise;
Whether to deck with clouds the uncolored sky,
Or wet the thirsty earth with falling showers,
Rising or falling, still advance his praise.

The Resurrection from Sleep

But it is yet more of a resurrection to you. Think of your own condition through the night and in the morning. You die, as it were, every night. The death of darkness comes down over the earth; but a deeper death, the death of sleep, descends on you. A power overshadows you; your eyelids close, you cannot keep them open if you would; your limbs lie moveless; the day is gone; your whole life is gone; you have forgotten everything; an evil man might come and do with your goods as he pleased; you are helpless.

But the God of the resurrection is awake all the time, watching his sleeping men and women, even as a mother who watches her sleeping baby, only with larger eyes and more full of love than hers; and so, you know not how, all at once you know that you are what you are; that there is a world that wants you outside of you, and a God that wants you inside of you; you rise from the death of sleep, not by your own power, for you know nothing about it; God put his hand over your eyes, and you were dead; he lifted his hand and breathed light on you, and you rose from the dead, thanked the God that raised you up, and went forth to do your work. From darkness to light; from blindness to seeing; from knowing nothing to looking abroad on the mighty world; from helpless submission to willing obedience—is not this a resurrection indeed?

That St. Paul saw it to be such may be shown from his using the two things with the same meaning when he says, "Awake, thou that sleepest, and arise from the dead, and Christ shall give thee light." No doubt he meant a great deal more. No man who understands what he is speaking about can well mean only one thing at a time.

Resurrections in Nature

But to return to the resurrections we see around us in nature. Look at the death that falls upon the world in winter. And look how it revives when the sun draws near enough in the spring to wile the life in it once more out of its grave. See how the pale, meek snowdrops come up with their bowed heads, as if full of the memory of the fierce winds they encountered last spring, and yet ready in the strength of their weakness to encounter them again. Up comes the crocus, bringing its gold safe from the dark of its colorless grave into the light of its parent gold. Primroses, and anemones, and blue-bells, and a thousand other children of the spring, hear the resurrection-trumpet of the wind from the west and south, obey, and leave their graves behind to breathe the air of the sweet heavens. Up and up they come till the year is glorious with the rose and lily, till the trees are not only clothed upon with new garments of loveliest green, but the fruit-tree bringeth forth its fruit, and the little children of men are made glad with apples, and cherries, and hazelnuts.

The earth laughs out in green and gold. The sky shares in the grand resurrection. The garments of its mourning, wherewith it made men sad, its clouds of snow and hail and stormy vapors, are swept away, have sunk indeed to the earth, and are now humbly feeding the roots of the flowers whose dead stalks they beat upon all the winter long. Instead, the sky has put on the garments of praise. Her blue, colored after the sapphire-floor on which stands the throne of him who is the Resurrection and the Life, is dashed and glorified with the pure white of sailing clouds, and at morning and evening prayer, puts on colors in which the human heart drowns itself with delight—green and gold and purple and rose. Even the icebergs, floating about in the lonely summer seas of the north, are flashing all the glories of the rainbow. But, indeed, is not this whole world itself a monument of the resurrection? The earth was without form and void. The wind of God moved on the face of the waters, and up arose this fair world. Darkness was on the face of the deep: God said, "Let there be light," and there was light.

Resurrection in the Animal World

In the animal world, as well, you behold the goings of the resurrection. Plainest of all, look at the story of the butterfly—so plain that the pagan Greeks called it and the soul by one name—Psyche. Psyche meant with them a butterfly or the soul, either. Look how the creeping thing, ugly to our eyes, so that we can hardly handle it without a shudder, finding itself growing sick with age, straightway falls a-spinning and weaving at its own shroud, coffin, and grave, all in one—to prepare, in fact, for its resurrection; for it is for the sake of the resurrection that death exists. Patiently it spins its strength, but not its life, away, folds itself up decently, that its body may rest in quiet till the new body is formed within it; and at length when the appointed hour has arrived, out of the body of this crawling thing breaks forth the winged splendor of the butterfly—not the same body—a new built out of the ruins of the old—even as St. Paul tells us that it is not the same body *we* have in the resurrection, but a nobler body like ourselves, with all the imperfect and evil thing taken away.

No more creeping for the butterfly; wings of splendor now. Neither yet has it lost the feet wherewith to alight on all that is lovely and sweet. Think of it—up from the toilsome journey over the low ground, exposed to the foot of every passer-by destroying the lovely leaves upon which it fed, and the fruit which they should shelter, up to the path at will through the air, and a gathering of food which hurts not the source of it, a food which is but as a tribute from the loveliness of the flowers to the yet higher loveliness of the flower-angel; is not this a resurrection? Its children too shall pass through the same process, to wing the air of a summer noon, and rejoice in the ethereal and the pure.

The Resurrection of the Body

I come now naturally to speak of what we commonly call the resurrection. Some say: "How can the same dust be raised again, when it may be scattered to the winds of heaven?" It is a question I hardly care to answer. The mere difficulty can in reason stand for nothing with God; but the apparent worthlessness of the supposition renders the question uninteresting to me. What is of import is, that I should stand clothed upon, with a body which is *my* body because it serves my ends, justifies my consciousness of identity by being, in all that was good in it, like that which I had before, while now it is tenfold capable of expressing the thoughts and feelings that move within me. How can I care whether the atoms that form a certain inch of bone should be the same as those which formed that bone when I died? All my lifetime I never felt or thought of the existence of such a bone! On the other hand, I object to having the same worn muscles, the same shriveled skin, with which I may happen to die. Why give me the same body as that? Why not rather my youthful body, which was strong, and facile, and capable? The matter in the muscle of my arm at death would not serve to make half the muscle I had when young.

But I thank God St. Paul says it will *not* be the same body. That body dies—up springs another body. I suspect myself that those are right who say that this body being the seed, the moment it dies in the soil of this world, that moment is the resurrection of the new body. The life in it rises out of it in a new body. This is not after it is put in the mere earth; for it is dead then, and the germ of life gone out of it. If a seed rots, no new body comes of it. The seed dies into a new life, and so does man. Dying and rotting are two very different things.

But I am not sure by any means. As I say, the whole question is rather uninteresting to me. What do I care about my old clothes after I have done with them? What is it to me to know what becomes of an old coat or an old pulpit-gown? I have no such clinging to the flesh. It seems to me that people believe their bodies to be themselves, and are therefore very anxious about them—and no wonder then. Enough for me that I shall have eyes to see my friends, a face that they shall know me by, and a mouth to praise God withal. I leave the matter with one remark, that I am well content to rise as Jesus rose, however that was. For me the will of God is so good that I would rather have his will done than my own choice given me.

The Resurrection Unto Life

But I now come to the last, because infinitely the most important, part of my subject—the resurrection for the sake of which all the other resurrections exist—the resurrection unto life. This is the one of which St. Paul speaks in my text. This is the one I am most anxious—indeed, the only one I am anxious to set forth, and impress upon you.

Think, then, of all the deaths you know; the death of the night, when the sun is gone, when friend says not a word to friend, but both lie drowned and parted in the sea of sleep; the death of the year, when winter lies heavy on the graves of the children of summer, when the leafless trees moan in the blasts from the ocean, when the beasts even look dull and oppressed, when the children go about shivering with cold, when the poor and improvident are miserable with suffering; or think of such a death of disease as befalls us at times, when the man who says, "Would God it were morning!" changes but his word, and not his tune, when the morning comes, crying, "Would God it were evening!" when what life is left is known to us only by suffering, and hope is among the things which were once and are no more—think of all these, think of them all together, and you will have but the dimmest, faintest picture of the death, from which the resurrection, of which I have now to speak, is the rising.

I shrink from the attempt, knowing how weak words are to set forth *the* death, set forth *the* resurrection. Were I to sit down to yonder organ, and crash out the most horrible dissonances that ever took shape in sound, I should give you but a weak figure of this death; were I capable of drawing from many a row of pipes an exhalation of dulcet symphonies and voices sweet, such as Milton himself could have invaded our ears withal, I could give you but a faint figure of this resurrection. Nevertheless, I must try what I can do in my own way.

If into the face of the dead body, lying on the bed, waiting for its burial, the soul of the man should begin to dawn again, drawing near from afar to look out once more at those eyes, to smile once again through those lips, the change on that face would be indeed great and wondrous, but nothing for marvel or greatness to that which passes on the countenance, the very outward bodily face of the man who wakes from his sleep, arises from the dead, and receives light from Christ.

Too often indeed, the reposeful look on the face of the dead body would be troubled, would vanish away at the revisiting of the restless ghost; but when a man's own right true mind, which God made in him, is restored to him again, and he wakes from the death of sin, then comes the repose without the death.

It may take long for the new spirit to complete the visible change, but it begins at once, and will be perfected. The bloated look of self-indulgence passes away like the leprosy of Naaman, the cheek grows pure, the lips return to the smile of hope instead of the grin of greed, and the eyes that made innocence shrink and shudder with their yellow leer grow childlike and sweet and faithful. The mammon-eyes, hitherto fixed on the earth, are lifted to meet their kind; the lips that mumbled over figures and sums of gold learn to say words of grace and tenderness. The truculent, repellent, self-satisfied face begins to look thoughtful and wistful, as if searching for some treasure of whose whereabouts it had no certain sign. The face, anxious, wrinkled, peering, troubled, on whose line you read the dread of hunger, poverty and nakedness, thaws into a smile; the eyes reflect in courage the light of the

Father's care; the back grows erect under its burden
with the assurance that the hairs of its head are all numbered.

From Selfishness to Love

But the face can with all its changes set but dimly
forth the rising from the dead which passes within. The
heart, which cared but for itself, becomes aware of surrounding thousands like itself, in the love and care of
which it feels a drawing blessedness undreamt of before. From selfishness to love—is not this a rising from
the dead? The man whose ambition declares that his
way in this world would be to subject everything to his
desires, to bring every human care, affection, power, and
aspiration to his feet—(such a world it would be, and
such a king it would have, if individual ambition might
work its will, if a man's opinion of himself could be
made out in the world, degrading, compelling, oppress-
ing, doing everything for his own glory, and such a
glory)—but a pang of light strikes this man to the heart;
an arrow of truth, feathered with suffering and loss and
dismay, finds out—the open joint in his armor, I was going to say—no, finds out the joint in the coffin where his
heart lies festering in a death so dead that itself calls it
life. He trembles, he awakes, he rises from the dead. No
more he seeks the slavery of all: where can he find whom
to serve? how can he become if but a threshold in the
temple of Christ, where all serve all, and no man thinks
first of himself?

He, to whom the mass of his fellows, as he massed
them, was common and unclean, bows before every human sign of the presence of the creating God. The sun
which was to him but a candle with which to search after
his own ends, wealth, power, place, praise—the world,
which was but the cavern where he thus searched—are

now full of the mystery of the loveliness, full of the truth of which sun and wind and land and sea are symbols and signs. From a withered old age of unbelief, the dim eyes of which refuse the glory of things a passage to the heart, he is raised up a child full of admiration, surprise, and gladness. Everything is glorious to him; he can believe, and therefore he sees. It is from the grave into the sunshine, from the night into the morning, from death into life.

To come out of the ugly into the beautiful; out of the mean and selfish into the noble and loving; out of the paltry into the great; out of the false into the true; out of the filthy into the clean; out of the commonplace into the glorious; out of the corruption of disease into the fine vigor and gracious movements of health; in a word, out of evil into good—is not this a resurrection indeed—*the* resurrection of all, the resurrection of life? God grant that with St. Paul we may attain to this resurrection of the dead!

This rising from the dead is often a long and a painful process. Even after he had preached the gospel to the Gentiles, and suffered much for the sake of his Master, Paul sees the resurrection of the dead towering grandly before him, not yet climbed, not yet attained unto—a mountainous splendor and marvel still shining aloft in the air of existence, still, thank God, to be attained, but ever growing in height and beauty as, forgetting those things that are behind, he presses towards the mark, if by any means he may attain to the resurrection of the dead.

Every blessed moment, in which a man bethinks himself that he has been forgetting his high calling, and sends up to the Father a prayer for aid; every time a man resolves that what he has been doing he will do no more; every time that the love of God, or the feeling of the truth, rouses a man to look first up at the light, then down at the skirts of his own garments—that moment a divine resurrection is wrought in the earth. Yea, every time that a man passes from resentment to forgiveness, from cruelty to compassion, from harshness to tenderness, from indifference to carefulness, from selfishness to honesty, from honesty to generosity, from generosity to love,—a resurrection, the bursting of a fresh bud of life out of the grave of evil, gladdens the eye of the Father watching his children.

Awake, then, thou that sleepest, and arise from the dead, and Christ will give the light! As the harvest rises from the wintry earth, so rise thou up from the trials of this world, a full ear in the harvest of him who sowed thee in the soil that thou mightest rise above it. As the summer rises from the winter, so rise thou from the cares of eating, and drinking, and clothing into the fearless sunshine of confidence in the Father. As the morning rises out of the night, so rise thou from the darkness of ignorance to do the will of God in the daylight; and as a man feels that he is himself when he wakes from the troubled and grotesque visions of the night into the glory of the sunrise, even so wilt thou feel that then first thou knowest what thy life, the gladness of thy being, is. As from painful tossing in disease, rise into the health of well-being. As from the awful embrace of thy own dead body, burst forth in thy spiritual body. Arise thou, responsive to the indwelling will of the Father, even as thy body will resound to the indwelling soul.

> White wings are crossing: glad waves are tossing;
>   The earth flames out in crimson and green:
> Spring is appearing, summer is nearing—
>   Where hast thou been?
>
> Down in some cavern, death's sleepy tavern,
>   Housing, carousing with spectres of night?
> The trumpet is pealing sunshine and healing—
>   Spring to the light!

⤾

"Divine and Human Relationship" originally appeared in The Christian World Pulpit. *MacDonald stresses in this sermon, as he does elsewhere, that it is obedience, and not just comprehension or theorization, that matters. We become the sons and daughters of God by being obedient to His will, and we learn obedience to God through our human relationships.*

CHAPTER THIRTEEN

Divine and Human Relationship

"For whosoever shall do the will of my Father which is in heaven, the same is my brother, and sister, and mother" (Matt. 12:50).

A little sad, was it not, that his mother and his brethren were not sitting about him? For, as another evangelist says, "he looked round on those that were about him." His disciples, who were learning of him, were nearest to him naturally, and his mother and his brethren were outside. They did not know him yet.

It takes a long time, and, what is more, a true heart, to know anybody. There are people that belong to the same family through the whole of a long life, and yet do not know each other to the very end. Do you remember they had set out to stop him? That is why they were outside; but for their stopping him they would have been at home. That lovely mother of his was not the first to understand him aright. Of course she understood him a good deal, and when the sword should have gone through her soul, she would understand him well. But there were other women, and they not so lovely as she, far less lovely in some ways, who understood him better, because the sword had passed through their souls, and

275

they knew the evil thing which brought them to his feet. These were outside desiring to speak to him, because they said, "He is beside himself." He was going too far, and they must stop him.

It was the necessity of his relations to see that he did not play the part of a madman. There are tens of thousands of so-called Christian people who are quite capable of doing the same thing at the present day, simply because they have little more of Christ in or about them than the common name that is given freely enough now, and is easy enough to carry. Nay, more, there are tens of thousands of those who are honest towards Christ, but yet know so little of what was in him or what he meant to do, that they would stop him.

It is a sad thing, friends, for any of us to be called by his name, and not know him. It is the business of our human being to know Christ, and nothing else is our business. If it is true that we are made into the image of God, the sole, paramount, all-including and absorbing business of existence is to know that image of God in which we are made, to know it in the living Son of God— the one only ideal man. The nearer I come to the change, the more absolutely I am convinced of this, and I have no words strong enough to put the statement in. But alas, for most of us, we like to pare away the words of Christ, instead of looking at them until they fill heaven and earth.

Christ's Mother and Brothers

Let us see what he meant in these lovely, awful, precious words. For the love of Christ is an awful thing. There is nothing in that which goes half way, or which makes exception. The Son of God loves so utterly that he will have his children clean, and if hurt and sorrow, pain and torture, will do to deliver any one of them from the horrible thing, from the death that he cherishes at the very root of his soul, the loving Christ, though it hurts him all the time, and though he feels every sting himself, will do it.

"Who are my mother and my brethren?" So he asks; and then he answers: "Whosoever does the will of my Father in heaven." You observe he is always talking about his Father in heaven. You would think he knew nothing else. He has but one word, as it seems, over and over again. It has been said that he was possessed with love for humanity, and that is true; but he was possessed before that, and as the beginning of that, with love to his Father in heaven. That was the root, the power, the energy of all that was manifest even in the eternal Son of God himself. It could not be otherwise. He was not to be misled with any outside shows of power and beauty. He knew the heart of them all, and that it was the living will of God, by which all things arose, subsisted, and went on growing and growing. The Father—the Father—the Father was all in all in the heart of the Son, and because the Father, therefore the children of the Father, all the men and women, savage and refined, throughout the universe.

And does it make us at all sorrowful that he said the words to his disciples, that he does not seem to include the rest of the company, and seems to exclude his mother and brethren? Is it a hard word, do you think? Oh, friends, the power of God himself can give you nothing worth having, but this that he would give, which the few about him had already taken, and which some of us have begun to take. Life is the only thing—life, that is the essential of well-being. It is because we are but half-alive now, half-created, you may say, and not nearly that, that we are not blessed. We so often choose death, the thing that separates and kills, for everything that parts us from our fellow, and everything that parts us from God, is a killing of us.

Whosoever is wide and free, and will do the will of

God—not understand it, not care about it, not theorize about it, but do it—is a son of God. It is in the act that man stands up as a son of God. He may be ever such a philosopher, ever such a theologian, ever such a patriot or benevolent man; but it is only he who, in the act, in the doing of the thing, stands up before God, that is a son of God. That is the divine dignity: "My Father worketh hitherto, and I work." It is he who works that is the son of God.

Do I mean outside works or inside works? I mean whatever a man does, whether it be the giving up all that he has to go and preach the gospel, or whether it be putting down the smallest rising thought of injustice, of anger and wrong, of selfishness in his soul. The act is where the will of man stands up against liking, against temptation, and leads him simply to do that which God would have him to do, easy or difficult; it may be to mount a throne, it may be to be sawn asunder. The man who does what God would have him do, what is he? "My brother," says Christ. The woman who does that? "My sister," says Christ. And as if he would go to the very depth of tenderness, he is not satisfied with saying "brother" or "sister." Woman, that has longed to have children and has none, did you ever think you might have a Son of God for your son? If you would be the "mother" of the Son of God, do the will of his Father, and yours and you will not mourn long.

Our Relationship to the Father

But was he putting away his mother? Was it an unkind, an unfilial thing to say? Did he, in saying, "Who is my mother, who is my brother?" repudiate the earthly mother and the earthly brother and sister? No, verily. But, friends, it is a profound, absolute fact that our relation to God is infinitely nearer than any relation by nature. Our mother does not make us; we come forth of her, but forth also of the very soul of God. We are nearer, unspeakably nearer, infinitely and unintelligibly (to our very poor intellects) nearer to God than to the best, loveliest, dearest mother on the face of the earth.

The Lord, first of all, only spake an absolute fact; but then he goes deeper and deeper still. This cannot be until the thing is known and acknowledged. But look: if a mother has two children, one of whom is as bad as a boy can be, and the other as good; the one is her child and the other is not her child; they are both born of her body, but the one that loves her and obeys her is born of her soul; yea, of her very spirit, and she says "This is my child," and she says to the other, with groans, "You are none of mine." And his being no child is the misery of the thing; she would die for the one who is no child, but for the one who is her child she would live forever.

And so when we become the sons and daughters of God indeed by saying, "Oh, my Father, I care for nothing but what thou carest for; I will not lament for this thing; because I see thou dost not care about it, I will not care either;" when you say, "This is sore to bear, but it is thy will, and therefore I thank thee for it, so sure am I of thy will, O my Father in heaven:" when we come to be able to talk like that, then we are in the same mind as Jesus Christ, whose delight, and whose only delight, was to do the will of his Father in heaven. But for God's sake, do not cling to your own poor will. It is not worth having. It is a poor, miserable, degrading thing to fall down and worship the inclination of your own heart, which may have come from any devil, or from any accident of your birth, or from the weather, or from anything. Take the will of God, eternal, pure, strong, living, and true, the only good thing; take that, and Christ will be your brother. If we knew the glory of that, I believe we could even delight in going against the poor small things that we should like in ourselves, delight even in thwarting ourselves.

Our Relationship to Our Parents

To return to my subject. Was Christ refusing his mother? Was he saying, "I come of another breed, and I have nothing to do with you?" Was that the spirit of it? The Son of God forbid! Never, never! But I must show here a deeper and a better thing. It is of the wisdom and tenderness of God that we come into the world as we do, that we form families, little centres, and groups of spiritual nerves and power in the world. I do not see how in any other way we come to understand God.

And, oh! you parents, who make it impossible for your children to understand God, what shall be said of or for you? If we had not fathers and mothers to love, I do not know how our hearts would understand God at all. I know not how I ever should. Then, again, if we had no brothers and sisters to love, how ever should we begin to learn this essential thing, that we should love our neighbor—that is, every man who comes near us to be affected with look or word—as ourselves?

It were an impossibility. God begins with us graciously and easily. He brings us near, first, to mother, then to father, then to sister, then to brother—brings us so near to them that we cannot escape them. The months of infancy and the years of childhood are unspeakably precious from this fact, that we cannot escape the holy influences of family. So many are our needs, so quiescent are our needs, that love is, as it were, heaped upon us and forced into us: and we are taught—as we cannot help learning—to love.

Our Relationship with Others

But woe to the man or woman who stops there, and can only love because the child, or the sister, or the brother is his or hers! The same human soul, the same hungry human affection, the same aspiring, although blotted and spoiled, human spirit, is within every head, dwelling in every heart, and we are brothers and sisters wherever God has made man or woman; and until we have learned that, we are only going on, it may be a little, to learn Christ, but we have not yet learned him. What! Shall Christ love a man, and I not love him? Shall Christ say to a woman, "My sister," and I not bow before her! It is preposterous. But then my own mother, my own father, my own brothers and sisters—if they be his too, they come first, they come nearer.

But I do assert that there is a closer, infinitely closer, relation between any one that loves God and any other that loves God, than there is between any child and any mother where they do not both love him. The one has its root, the other has its leaves and flowers as well. We cannot love anybody too much; but we do not, we can never, love our own child aright until we have learned to love— not the mildness of the child—but the humanity of the child, the goodness, the thing that God meant, that came out of his will. That is the thing we have to love even in our children, or else the love is a poor dying thing, because we ourselves are dying. I am supposing that we do not possess the love of God, which is the only eternal thing. But if we love God, dearer and dearer grow the faces of father and mother, wife and child, until there is no end to it. It goes on, not only eternally in time, but eternally in growth, expanding. We do not understand it, because we are no farther on.

Every bit we get farther, we understand more, and perceive more, and feel more; and the child of God is infinite, because he is a child of God. The child is like the Father. We have our share in God's infinitude, and therefore the Lord Christ himself called us "gods" when he quoted from the Psalms. Whoever can, let him understand the words, "I say, ye are gods." The children of

God must be gods in some sense. Little gods, indeed, but what is their completion and salvation? "Ye shall sit down with me in my throne, even as I am set down with my Father in his throne." And brothers and sisters, I cannot conceive any other sufficing redemption than this, that we should be set down on the throne of the King of kings, with the Lord our Master, as he said. Do you call this presumption? I appeal to Christ, for he has spoken. I believe in nothing but Christ; and so I trust to believe everything that is true, to know it when I see it.

Claiming Christ

Are you lonely? Has lover or friend forsaken you? Has death taken father or mother, husband or wife, sister or brother from you? If you could see aright, that is a trifle; a profound trifle, though, for God's trifles are precious and great. Dear in the sight of God is the death of his saints. But it is a trifle. I will tell you what would be the terrible thing. Have you been false to them? Have you wronged them? Have you been such that there has been a separation, a tearing of your souls asunder? That is death, and the devil, and damnation. Why is it death that we fear? He hath abolished death. He died and he was not dead; up he rose again radiant with light and victory. So are they all who believe in him; for he said, "He that liveth and believeth in me shall never die." You may defy death. Only have the "patience of Christ;" there is given us that phrase; wait in his name and you shall have all you want. For when Christ has had his way with you, you would as soon ask for anything that he did not like as you would beg of God to destroy the universe he had created. There would be nothing to you desirable that is not desirable in his eyes.

Think of this: that you can have One who is more than brother or sister, father or mother, husband or wife, or child,—One from whose heart all these flowed out—One from whom came the love that analyzed itself into these forms because of its infinitude. You can have him for your own friend, for brother, sister, mother, son. Whatever relation is possible in humanity, that relation does the heart of Christ feel to every one that can take it.

Do you want, therefore, to forget, and take Christ as a make-up for the others that are gone? Never! never! That is not his way. For how constantly does he tell you to love one another? That is the glory of Christ's teaching; that is his gospel; there is not an atom of selfishness in God, or in Christ, for he delights to see us loving one another. He cannot be satisfied except by seeing us love each other perfectly—that is his delight. Nay, more than this, I repeat, we cannot love one of our own aright unless Christ is in us making us love that person to the idea of that relationship. Never father loved child, never child loved father, to the idea of fatherhood and childhood, unless Christ was not only born in him but had grown up in him; and in none has he grown to that degree that he understands thoroughly, feels thoroughly, believes thoroughly—or anything like thoroughly—any relation in life, so far as I know.

Do not take from the glory of the words of Christ; do not be afraid to claim from him what he gives you, and would have you take. Claim him, man, woman, boy, girl, claim him as your own; for without him you are as nothing. Claim him, by taking the will of God for your one care, your one object, your one desire; and Christ will be yours altogether. "Behold I stand at the door, and knock: if any man hear my voice, and open the door, I will come in to him, and will sup with him, and he with me."

Partaking of the same food together—that food being the very will of God: "it is my meat and drink to do thy will:" that is the very food concerning which our Lord says: "man shall not live by bread alone, but by every word that proceedeth out of the mouth of God." That is the will of God; it is the very food and drink of the true heart; and when Jesus and the man who has opened to him the door sit down together, it is to share together in the understanding of the will of the Father of both—that Father to whom he went when he said: "Go to my brethren, and say unto them, I ascend unto my Father, and your Father; and to my God and your God."